DO YOU KNOW . . .

- How to foster your child's creativity?

- When your Two-Year-Old should be able to balance on one foot . . . stand on tiptoe . . . ride a tricycle?

- How to help your child develop important concepts such as time, consequences, and classification?

- Whether or not to correct your child's mispronunciation of words?

- What play rules a Two-Year-Old can follow?

- What to do when a Two-Year-Old deliberately disobeys you?

- How to help your child express angry feelings without hitting or hurting others?

- Whether or not to start teaching a bright Two-Year-Old to read and write?

Don't miss any of the helpful, caring advice about the issues you will face at this important stage of your child's life!

·THE MAGICAL YEARS·

Surviving Your
TWO-YEAR-OLD

Janet Poland

Judi Craig, Ph. D.,
Consulting Editor

A Skylight Press Book

ST. MARTIN'S PAPERBACKS

Published by arrangement with Skylight Press, 260 West 72nd Street, Suite 6-C, New York, N.Y. 10023, (212) 874-4348.

THE MAGICAL YEARS:
SURVIVING YOUR TWO-YEAR-OLD

ISBN: 0-312-95582-0

Printed in the United States of America

St. Martin's Paperbacks edition/August 1995

10 9 8 7 6 5 4 3 2 1

Contents

Introduction

Who can think of two-year-olds without the expression "terrible twos" popping into mind? The balkiness, the constant "No"s, the tantrums, the hazards of toilet training—this infamous stage of a child's life signals the beginnings of power struggles in many parents' minds!

But there's MUCH more to your child this year, as *Surviving Your Two-Year-Old* will attest. Janet Poland does a fine job of describing basic developmental issues in the child of 24 to 36 months, giving the reader many glimpses of the joy and delight a two-year-old can bring into a parent's life *in addition* to the occasional frustration that can result from the toddler's beginning ventures toward independence.

Rather than a dry, textbookish discussion of a child's changing abilities physically, intellectually, socially and emotionally, Poland makes these changes come to life with everyday, often humorous examples. She helps the reader understand the two-year-old's world through the two-year-old's eyes, language and moods.

Poland also tackles the important issue of limit-setting, helping a parent lay a sound foundation for positive discipline. This is nicely balanced by discussion of a toddler's need to be allowed some reasonable choices, encouraging the kind of parental flexibility that produces healthy psychological development. She then leads the reader into the daily routines of the typical two's life, including waking up, dressing, eating, napping, bathing, toileting, and going to bed.

Taking into account today's interest in diet and nutrition, Poland addresses it as it applies to toddlers. Not only does she give tips about specific food choices, she presents a sound rationale for the prevention of eating hassles.

A must for every parent, *Surviving Your Two-Year-Old* includes a marvelous chapter on how to make the world of a toddler a safe place to be. Whether it's the child's own room, the family living area, the kitchen, the bathroom, outdoor areas (including swimming pools), the car, or a youngster's toys, safety-conscious parents will appreciate the specific recommendations and tips for each subject.

Surviving Your Two-Year-Old's easy-to-read format includes a general view of each chapter's theme plus a practical "How to Help" guide for parents. Chapters conclude with "Time Capsules," giving an instant overview of what to expect in the child at 24, 30 and 36 months related to the chapter's topic, along with commonly asked questions about problem situations and options for solutions.

Whether the task at hand is getting teeth brushed, helping to settle squabbles in playgroup, introducing the potty, dealing with bedtime routine, encouraging language development, or managing tantrum behavior, *Surviving Your Two-Year-Old* provides simple, clear guidelines for the parent who's wanting to make the "terrible two's" not terrible at all!

Judi Craig, Ph.D.
Clinical Psychologist, Author & Speaker

·THE MAGICAL YEARS·

Surviving Your
TWO-YEAR-OLD

1

Welcome to My World

Your Two-Year-Old is, or soon will be, a study in contradictions: between his babyish self and his child self, between pleasing you and asserting himself, between being a delight to be around and behaving like a little terror.

He also has a contradictory reputation. You've probably heard the knowing chuckles from other parents about having a Two-Year-Old—the naughtiness, the fussiness, the tantrums.

There's plenty of substance behind that reputation, of course. But it's by no means the entire picture. There's much more to a Two-Year-Old than meets the eye.

"When my daughter was One, she was such a joy. Nothing seemed to faze her. She just bumbled along, never seemed to care what was going on around her. She was so easy to amuse—a cracker and a toy was all she needed. Everything was 'no problem.'

"Now she's Two, and everything has changed. She's so much more in tune with what's going on around her, and she's sensitive to our moods. She orders us around like a little general. It seems like nothing is ever just right. If she gets a chocolate ice-cream cone, she cries because it's not strawberry. She's like Goldilocks before she gets to the Baby Bear's porridge. Everything is too hot, too cold, or she can't make up her mind. It makes me nostalgic for One!''

Yet the father of a different Two-Year-Old sees the year quite differently: ''I know the 'Terrible Twos' have a bad reputation, but I think it's great. My son is more fun to be with, and we can sort of reason with him to keep him out of trouble. He's excited about everything and wants to tell us what he sees, what he's doing. He's starting to ask questions. If something is bothering him, he can pretty much tell us what's on his mind. He's a pleasure to be around.''

This year, despite some rough patches along the road, your Two-Year-Old, too, will become good company, even more so than he is now. Already, your child is his own person, and you know him well. You know his likes and dislikes, what frightens him, what calms him, what makes him giggle. If your Two-Year-Old is your first child, you begin to appreciate that you have another full-fledged member of your family.

He's eager to learn about the world, and it's a world full of new and wonderful things. You will be part of his process of discovery, and he will turn to you for explanations, interpretations, and reassurance.

He's not only learning about rules and expectations and limits, he's also beginning to understand that he is an individual with choices about whether or not to obey those rules and comply with those expectations. He is developing that glorious yet complex human character-istic called free will. He will practice exercising it, at first in unacceptable ways. Your job this year is to help him direct this will in positive directions, and help him remain curious about the world and proud of his new-found self.

SEEING THE WORLD THROUGH HIS EYES

The world of the Two-Year-Old is shimmering and new. Last year, his senses absorbed a wealth of detail: the taste of an orange, the weight of a stone, the feel of a kitten, the sound of your voice. Over time, he attached words to things and characteristics, and learned to reach out to you with words as well as with his arms.

This year, the world is still shimmering and new, but it is a bigger world because his ability to think has extended its boundaries. Now his world contains dump trucks and elephants, Big Bird and clocks, snowsuits and caterpillars and clouds. And it includes red, blue, fast, slow, hot, cold, yesterday, soon. It includes memories of last weekend's ice-cream cone and anticipation of tomorrow's trip to the beach.

His world is expanding so much, however, that it throws him off balance. Last year, he had to learn to walk steadily on two feet. This year, he has to learn to bring his thoughts and his language and his memory and his impulses into some kind of balance. The bigger his world becomes, the smaller he senses he is. The more he learns about the world's complexities, the more bewildered he becomes. The more he learns about powerful forces such as thunder and dinosaurs and the anger of a parent, the more aware he is of his own vulnerability.

Because his understanding is so limited, he sees the

3

world as full of magic, and sometimes full of monsters. His curiosity draws him into this enchanted realm to investigate and wonder and ask questions, but his sense of vulnerability drives him to seek out reassurance in the familiar. Sometimes comfort comes in the form of a rigid insistence on sameness: the same blanket at bedtime, the same story read just the same way.

His greatest comfort comes from his attachment to you. He is beginning to understand what pleases you and what angers you, and he wants to remain in your good graces. And yet he must risk your anger and disapproval from time to time if he is to grow. His understanding of rules and expectations is increasing, but he is driven to push himself beyond these rules. Just as he tore pages out of books and stretched his Slinky out of shape last year to test the limits of materials, this year he tests other limits: He pulls another child's hair to see what she'll do, and what you'll do. Or he creeps into the kitchen when you're trying to get dinner on the table and grabs for knives, just to see how far he can push you.

UNIVERSAL THEMES

In the following chapters, we'll look at how your child is growing and developing this year, and focus on the fundamental tasks that he must accomplish: learning to communicate, learning to behave within reasonable limits, learning to care for himself in more mature ways. And we'll discuss ways to feed him and help him feed himself, and how to keep him safe.

Physical Development

Physically, your Two-Year-Old will continue on the path set last year: his body will grow fairly slowly, and his energy level will remain high. This will be a time of refining his skills. All his furious physical activity will have the effect of strengthening his muscles and his coordination, and by Three, he will move with grace and control. No longer the waddling toddler, he will be an agile child.

Intellectual Growth

Your child's mind will develop dramatically as he expands his understanding of time and space. He'll begin to understand past and future, and use words that reflect that understanding. His memory will improve, as will his recognition of cause and effect, so he will begin to reason, and to plan, and to think about what he's doing.

Language

You'll see your child's thought process reflected in his exploding powers of speech, as he tells you all about what he's doing and joins in your conversations. His grammar, while decidedly primitive, will be logically consistent. His speech will be refreshingly literal and will demonstrate how he thinks about things (and provide you with amusement as well): When you say that Aunt Susan is going to fly to Miami, he may question you, pointing out that Aunt Susan doesn't have any wings.

Social Growth

Your Two-Year-Old will extend his social world beyond himself and his immediate family and begin to make overtures toward other children and develop comfortable relationships with other adults. His interest in social interaction will probably outpace his skills, and you will have much to teach him. His play sessions with other children probably will not always go smoothly. More than anything, he needs practice (in appropriate supervised settings) and he needs time to mature. By Three, he'll be learning to share, beginning to consider the feelings of others, and forming true friendships.

Emotions

Because he will be able to talk to you more, you will have a bigger window into your child's emotional life this year. He will express his affection and his delight in words, and not just in giggles. He will also express his anger and fear verbally. Even as his fears become more imaginative, his ability to be comforted by ideas— and your reassuring words—will keep pace.

Setting Limits

This is a crucial year for establishing reasonable expectations for your child's behavior. Unlike last year, your Two-Year-Old is growing more aware of his own actions and their consequences, and he is learning ways to get what he wants. If this year he learns that whining, howling, or grabbing are the most effective ways, this behavior will be difficult to correct later. This is the year to teach some social norms, set some firm limits, and establish patterns of cooperation. Despite your best efforts, you will probably see more tantrums than last year, and plenty of testing and outright defiance. If you learn to work with him, rather than just against him, by year's end you will be rewarded with a much more congenial Three-Year-Old.

Daily Routines

This year, your Two-Year-Old will become an active participant in his own care. He will thrive on a sense of order and ritual about everything from where he positions his rocking horse to which bowl his cereal is served in. He will want the same story (or lots of stories) read just the same way, no word omitted, every night. He will quickly catch on to the daily schedule, and anticipate when Mom or Dad is due to come home and where you keep your purse or car keys. All of this provides him with immense reassurance and comfort. This is the year, also, that many children make the major shift from diapers to toilet. You'll need to watch your Two-Year-Old for signs of readiness, and be ready to begin the process or wait until later, according to the signals he gives you.

Food and Nutrition

As was the case last year, your child probably will not have the vigorous appetite he had as a baby. However, he will have strong opinions about what foods he likes and dislikes. He still may be fussy and particular, but his balkiness can be handled in such a way that you retain your sanity and he gets the nourishment he needs. He will develop skills in using a knife and fork and eating more neatly.

Keeping Him Safe

As he matures intellectually and becomes more willing to follow rules, your child will be better able to keep himself out of harm's way. However, the burden is still essentially yours. Even though your Two-Year-Old obeys safety rules some of the time, that doesn't mean he'll obey at any specific time—or that he even will remember the rules on a particular occasion. So you will still need to use childproofing techniques and constant vigilance to protect him.

THE POWER OF PLAY

The primary force that motivates your Two-Year-Old is your love. But if there's any one thing that drives him forward developmentally, it's his experience in play.

It's through active play that your child becomes physically strong this year. It's through play that he learns the properties of the world, and masters ever more complex concepts of time, space, numbers, and cause and effect. Word play and fun songs help him practice his burgeoning language skills, and play—with other children and with you—gives him practice in relating to other people.

He'll need safe spaces where he can play freely with materials, with other children, with paper and crayons. He'll need play experiences and materials that are unstructured, ones that are motivated by his own interests, not the interests of an adult. You may be tempted to buy the latest luxury toy advertised on television, but the chances are that this year he'll get more pleasure from ordinary wooden blocks.

Throughout this book, we'll suggest play activities and materials that will help your child develop his body, his mind, his feelings, and his social skills.

WHAT TO EXPECT, OVER TIME

Most of the following chapters (the ones that deal essentially with development rather than technique) end with a short summary, or "Time Capsule," of what you can expect at three stages of this year. These stages (24, 30, and 36 months) refer very loosely to the early, middle, and final months of the year. This breakdown is helpful because your child will change so much during the year that the Two-Year-Old you sing Happy Birthday to today will be a very different creature by the time you add another candle to the cake.

At twenty-four months, your toddler is probably walking fairly well, but not entirely gracefully. He may be able to talk to you in sentences, and he certainly understands you when you speak to him. His ability to remember and anticipate are just beginning to increase, and he uses words to express abstractions like "soon" or "up," along with his growing vocabulary of nouns and verbs. He still prefers your company, and although he is interested in other children, he doesn't yet know how to approach them or respond appropriately. He expresses a full range of emotions. He is fairly compliant and eager to please. He is learning to do more for himself, and his body is growing more ready for toileting later in the year.

At midyear, the legendary Terrible Twos make their appearance. This is when testing behavior, defiance, and rigid demands can make your little one difficult to live with. His physical strength and stamina are improving, and he is more in control of his movements. He may be able to scribble and manipulate puzzle pieces. His memory is improving, and his understanding of time and space are growing more refined. His increasing ability to think is reflected in his speech. He takes what you say literally, but he describes his world creatively. His interest in other children will increase, and he will be more eager to play with others. Your child's abilities, however, won't match his interest; when thirty-month-olds get together, play often degenerates into chaos. Your toddler will be more rigid and resistant than ever at midyear, more demanding of a precise bedtime ritual, and more likely to test your limits.

Toward year's end, most Two-Year-Olds are beginning to emerge from the ferment of midyear. Physically, your child will be much more agile and capable than he was at just Two. He will start to draw pictures and tell you what they are. He will talk much more to his playmates, and involve them in imaginative and pretend play. His growing imaginative abilities may increase his fears, and he may have more nightmares. He will grow more agreeable to rules and limits, and his testing behavior will diminish. He will be easier to manage as he grows more flexible in his routines. He may well be ready to use the toilet on his own, and he will be able to care for himself—from dressing to washing his hands—more independently.

NO TWO ALIKE

Of course the developmental stages outlined in this book are averages, and won't match every Two-Year-Old's development. And the road that children travel this year is not straight and smooth; it's full of rocky places, detours, and occasional backtracks.

We'll talk about the difficulty of managing a Two-Year-Old at midyear, yet you may have a thirty-month-old Miss Congeniality who's a cheerful team player. We'll talk about the Two's improving abilities with dressing and using eating utensils, but you may have a little Pig Pen on your hands. Some children don't speak in understandable sentences until well into the year. Some may seem to master the use of the potty and then do a complete about-face. Some, believe it or not, stay sweet and cooperative all year long and never get into the testing, defiant stages described here.

Your Two-Year-Old is unlike any other Two-Year-Old who has ever gone before him. People are unique, partly because of genetic differences that affect physical and intellectual development as well as temperament. And gender plays a role; girls seem to reach most developmental milestones a bit sooner than boys.

So don't take the timing of the developmental milestones that we mention here too seriously. Instead of comparing and worrying, read ahead to see what new adventure might be coming up next. After all, with so much happening this year you don't want to miss anything.

FINDING THE RIGHT FIT

Of course, if your Two-Year-Old is unique, then so are his parents. You'll need to take the suggestions from this book and tailor them to your own personal style, your history, your philosophy. Some of the suggestions may have to be modified to suit your own personal thresholds for noise and clutter, not to mention your life style, your schedule, and your level of patience.

In matters of discipline, for example, your own childhood experience may affect the limits you set for your child and how you enforce them. You may find it hard to deny your child anything, or to say "No" and make it stick. Or you may find yourself bristling when your Two-Year-Old "talks back," because you were brought up to speak respectfully.

And that's as it should be. Raising a child is as much an art as a science. It's not the mechanical details—such as the ounces of carrots consumed or the minutes in a Time-Out—that matter in the grand scheme of things. It's not whether you are patient or high-strung, tidy or not-so-tidy. What counts is the broad picture, the tapestry you weave thread by thread, day by day, as you fill your child's life with fun, affection, guidance, and comfort.

Over the course of a year, the way you manage the daily challenges of living with a Two-Year-Old will shape the relationship you have with your child for years to come. It's the cumulative effect of all your actions that will teach him how to get along with other people, and what's expected in civilized company. The more you know about his developmental tasks, and the more you are able to see the world through his eyes, the more effective you'll be as a parent.

In the twinkling of an eye, the challenging parts of this year will be gone. Yet the delightful parts will be over as well. So don't be in too much of a hurry—before you know it, you will stand with your child on the threshold of the preschool years.

2

Playing to Her Strengths: Physical Growth and Development

Two-Year-Old Sarah is at the zoo with her parents. She rushes from one cage to another, enthralled by tigers and elephants. She laughs at the monkeys and watches the coiled python with wary fascination.

Sarah's enjoyment of this outing is a pleasant surprise for her parents. "Last time we came, she pretty much ignored the animals," Sarah's father recalls. "She paid more attention to the water fountains than she did to the bears. And after about half an hour, she got tired and wanted to be carried.

"But this time, she's so much more interested. And she's a lot stronger now. She just motors along, keeping up with us. It's fun to do things together. We feel like a threesome now."

Sarah, like most Two-Year-Olds, is indeed a stronger and more capable physical being than she was at One. She walks and runs more like a child than an infant. She tires less quickly. This year, she will continue some of her One-Year-Old patterns, such as a fairly slow rate of growth and a high energy level. But all her bustling activity will help her master skills at a rapid rate until, at age Three, she becomes an agile, graceful preschooler.

HIGHLIGHTS OF PHYSICAL DEVELOPMENT

Let's take a look at some of the physical progress your Two-Year-Old will make this year:

- She will continue her slow, steady growth, gaining about two or three inches in height and about four or five pounds. American boys average about 34.5 inches at age Two, 37.5 inches at age Three. The average weight is about 28 pounds at Two, 32 pounds at Three. For girls, the average height is about 34 inches at Two, 37 at Three; weight averages about 26 pounds at Two, 31 pounds at Three.
- You will see more variability in height and weight this year. The tallest children will be dramatically taller than the shortest children, even though all may fall within the range of normal.
- Between the second and third birthday, a toddler's appearance grows more "child"-like as proportions change. Arms and legs grow more than the head and torso. Even as your child adds several inches overall, her "sitting height" increases only slightly.
- The brain is growing more slowly and, by year's end, will approach its adult size.
- Your child's senses continue to develop, and grow more precise and acute. Eyes move and rotate well,

and both distant and close-range focus are sharp. Peripheral vision improves as well.

- Her body gradually grows leaner, as fat is replaced by muscle and bone. Cheeks become less round; even the pads on the arches of the feet decrease, making feet less "flat."
- Her patterns of sleep mature, as she needs slightly less sleep overall and fewer daytime naps.
- Her patterns of digestion and elimination also mature; her bowels move at more regular times during the day, increasing her readiness for toilet learning. Control of sphincter muscles that regulate the release of urine and feces usually develops during the first half of this year. Your Two-Year-Old is now able to retain urine for several hours; you'll notice that she is frequently dry after naptime (but rarely when she awakens in the morning).
- By now, she probably has all her baby teeth. It's time to make dental hygiene one of her routines (see Chapter 8). It's also time to take her to the dentist for a checkup, since tooth decay is common in toddlers. It's best to have her see the dentist before she needs any kind of treatment, so her first experience is a pleasant one. If possible, choose a dentist who specializes in the treatment of young children. Pediatric dentists are expert at preventing and alleviating fears.

GROSS MOTOR DEVELOPMENT

"When Elizabeth turned Two last summer," recalls the mother of a very active little girl, "I had this idea that she might slow down a bit and I'd actually get some

17

use out of my hammock! But I guess that will have to wait. She still goes full blast from morning to night.''

Of course Two-Year-Olds vary in their activity level, but most continue their love affair with motion and activity that began when they learned to walk. This year, however, there will be some important changes in the way toddlers use their bodies and their boundless energy.

At thirty months of age, Elizabeth focuses her energies much more than she did last year. At eighteen months, for example, she would climb everything she could—the couches, the stairs, even the kitchen counter by way of the stools ranged around it. She would empty all the drawers she could reach, for the sheer pleasure of emptying things. She would run almostly blindly from one fleeting activity to another, sometimes bumping into walls.

Now, at thirty months, Elizabeth begins the morning by picking up her stuffed panda and heading for her favorite toy, a large plastic kiddie car. She puts the panda in the seat next to her, slams the door, and begins a journey that includes frequent stops, getting in and out, dropping off and picking up the panda, and various other pickups and deliveries. During about ten minutes of this activity, Elizabeth provides a running commentary: ''Go over here. Zoom, zoom, gonna get ice cream. Okay, Panda, gotta get out. . . . Here's your ice cream. . . .''

When Elizabeth and her mother go for a walk, she actually walks—unlike most One-Year-Olds, who consider walks to be nonlinear events, with more side trips and dawdles than actual forward motion. Now, she enjoys the walk itself and the idea of walking to someplace. Along the way, she jumps, walks backward, hops. She climbs, when a convenient wall or porch step beckons, but often even her climbing has a purpose—she wants to see what's on the other side of the wall.

Elizabeth's energy is more focused, and her activity, although pleasurable in itself, frequently has a goal. Now, when she empties a basket of blocks, it's because she intends to sit down and build with them.

And the way Elizabeth moves has changed, too. No longer does she stagger along with her hands held out for balance, charging straight ahead. Now she walks with a child's gait and a practiced, heel-toe step. She runs skillfully, climbs surefootedly, and falls less (although she still gets her share of skinned knees). She even varies her method of walking, as if she's mastered the basics and wants to make things interesting: She tries walking backward or sideways, hops on two feet, walks stiff-legged like a stick figure, dances. She still can't skip, however; that rather complex skill will take a year or more to develop.

The Gross Motor Accomplishments

- During this year, your child may begin to walk up stairs with alternating feet, rather than one step at a time. She will learn this skill going upstairs before she can manage it going downstairs.
- She will be able to stand on tiptoe and balance on one foot.
- She will be able to run and jump with greater coordination, although her control of stopping and turning will not be complete yet.

- She'll be able to throw, catch, and kick a large ball without losing balance.

The Importance of Physical Activity

Your Two-Year-Old's bounding physical activity and energy is not just inevitable, it's also essential.

- She needs physical activity as an outlet for all her energy.
- All her running, climbing, dancing, wiggling, and squirming strengthens her muscles.
- Her agility, coordination, and balance improve this year partly because she is maturing neurologically, but also as a result of practice.
- Whether it's balancing on a board or climbing one rung higher on the jungle gym, her mastery of physical skills builds her confidence and makes her more eager for other challenges.

How to Help

- Provide an uncluttered play space for free and rough-and-tumble play. A playroom or fenced area of the yard should be free of hazards and cleared of "don't touch" items.
- Take part in active play. Your child will love piggy-back rides, chase games, and simple hiding and finding games.
- Jungle gyms, inclines, tunnels, and low balance beams are fun and provide excellent practice. Make sure

climbing structures are safe and low. If your Two-Year-Old climbs on structures higher than she is, an adult should supervise.

- She'll enjoy swinging, but probably will need to be pushed at first.
- Transportation toys are great favorites. Small trucks are wonderful for rolling and pushing and transporting other objects, and big kiddie cars provide opportunities for solo trips, giving rides, and pushing.
- Provide large blocks for construction play. Hollow box-type blocks are great for building walls, barriers, houses, roads, and forts. Have enough so that your child can build a satisfying structure without always running short of blocks.
- Rocking horses should be low enough for a child to mount and dismount on her own.
- A playhouse encourages active social play, as does child-size furniture, such as tables, movable chairs, and kitchen appliances.
- Remember that girls as well as boys need all the physical, social, and emotional benefits of vigorous physical play. If you have a daughter, or have girls in your toddler play group, give them the same freedom to be physical, loud, and messy that you give boys.
- Dress your Two-Year-Old in clothing appropriate for rough-and-tumble play. Don't restrict her with tight, uncomfortable, or too-fancy clothing when it's time to let off steam.

FINE MOTOR DEVELOPMENT

The busy bee quality of Two-Year-Olds is not limited, happily, to whole-body activity. Their hands and fingers are just as busy testing, poking, fitting, squishing, and continuing their exploration of the physical world.

Andrew, at thirty-three months, is beginning to show some of the typical acceleration of fine motor mastery that often becomes evident in the second half of this year. He has shifted his crayon grasp from the babyish overhand grip he used before to the adult grasp that uses the thumb. His scribbling is not representational, although he likes to make curved lines and circles. He loves toys that fit together, and he is learning to string large beads.

Andrew hasn't yet perfected his coordination and control in the use of his hands. That's the end toward which all his fiddling and playing are moving. He's adept at taking apart his pop-it beads, but it takes him longer to put them back together. When Andrew is carrying a truck in his hand and sees an interesting book, he drops the truck unceremoniously to the floor and goes after the book.

Yet he sits at the piano with his father, touches a tiny forefinger to the keys with great delicacy and control, and delights in the sound he makes.

In contrast to last year, your Two-Year-Old spends more time on each activity, so there is less seemingly random flitting about. She's more likely than last year to sit down with a book, work on a puzzle, or draw for a few moments.

. There is, of course, great variation in the temperament and energy level of toddlers. But even Elizabeth will settle down a bit as she hones her fine motor skills.

The Fine Motor Accomplishments

- Your Two-Year-Old's control of her hands, her grasp and release, and the ability to use her fingers individually—rather than together—will continue to improve this year.
- She will make ever taller towers out of her blocks. At the beginning of this year, she will probably be able to pile up about six or eight blocks; by the time she is Three she may be able to make a skyscraper of eight or more blocks.
- She will become adept at the twisting motions involved in unscrewing lids and opening doors.
- She will become better at manipulating utensils at mealtime, opening containers, and dressing herself.
- Early in the year, her scribbles will be primitive. Most likely, she will make vertical lines before she can make horizontal ones, and lines before she makes circles. Later in the year, she will learn to connect her scribbling efforts with their results. She may agree, when she's finished, that she's drawn a rainbow, but she probably didn't start out intending it to be a rainbow. At twenty-four months, she probably won't be interested in scribbling for more than a few minutes,

but by year's end she may sit and draw happily for fifteen minutes.

BUT IS IT ART?

Recently, Kyle invited another Two-Year-Old over for a morning's play. Kyle's mother got out a variety of art supplies, including colored paper, tape, and clay.

After half an hour of this activity, all the tape was gone, but none had actually been used to tape anything together. The paper had been reduced to confetti. And the clay, after being rolled into balls, was used as cannonballs and was now mostly sticking to the walls.

"I had this idea that they'd have fun making things," Kyle's mother said with a sigh. "But I guess they have more fun just kind of messing around."

And indeed they do, especially early in the year. Despite the pleasure that many Two-Year-Olds take in scribbling and painting, when it comes to arts and crafts, they still are more interested in the process and the qualities of the materials than they are with any finished product. So by all means provide your Two-Year-Old with a chance to have artistic experiences. But you may not end up with too many masterpieces to frame just yet.

PLAYTHINGS FOR LITTLE FINGERS

Two-Year-Olds need ample opportunity to manipulate objects and experiment with the properties of materials, just as they did last year. This year, however, the objects can be more refined and require more skill, and they can take on more symbolic value as children apply their budding imagination to their playthings.

It's a lot of fun to watch a playful Two-Year-Old enjoying herself with a puzzle or set of little cars. But fight the temptation to rush out and buy her toys that are too advanced or difficult to handle. If she can't put the pieces together, or pull them apart, she will become frustrated.

Remember, also, the importance of unstructured play for a Two-Year-Old. As her ability to think symbolically increases, so does her ability to make objects "be" whatever she wants them to be. A plain block can be anything from a house to a horse to a sandwich. But a fancy, highly detailed toy or game that can only do one thing is likely to grow stale quickly. You want your child to develop her own imagination and creativity, not just follow some play objective dreamed up by an adult.

Recommended for Twos:

- Blocks, wooden or plastic, in several sizes and shapes.
- Large wooden beads and a metal-tipped lace to string them on.
- Small plastic or wooden figures—people, farm animals, vehicles. Commercial cartoon figures are fun, but include some "generic" figures too—plain men, women, children, horses, tigers. Make sure little figures and their accessories pass the "tube test" for prevention of choking hazards (See Chapter 10 for details). Fisher-Price, for example, has recently updated its "Little People" sets so the figures are large enough for toddlers.
- Inset boards and jigsaw puzzles with five or fewer

pieces early this year, and increasing to six to twelve by year's end. Early in the year, puzzles with knobs on the pieces are helpful because they make it easier for little fingers to take them out.

- Arts and crafts supplies: Clay or Play-Doh, fingerpaint, crayons and blank paper, paste and construction paper. Try offering one kind of material at a time (precut paper and paste today, paper and crayons tomorrow), and don't expect tidiness or a strong artistic vision on the part of your Two-Year-Old.

- Especially after midyear, many Two-Year-Olds are able to handle a paintbrush (at least a half-inch wide) and poster paints, and work happily at an easel. The process is more fun for Twos than the finished product. Don't interfere or "show how" too much.

- Plain paper and crayons. While it's fun to introduce your child to a whole rainbow of crayons, and use drawing time to try to teach colors, you might want to, occasionally, offer one dark color and white paper, so her attention is on the shapes and patterns she is creating, rather than on the crayons themselves.

- Depending on your Two-Year-Old's habits, you may need to keep crayons and art supplies put away, to be used when you can supervise. Many a Two-Year-Old can't resist becoming a graffiti artist or muralist.

- Blank paper is preferable to coloring books.

- A sandbox, dirt pile, or area for contained water play is heaven for a Two-Year-Old. Be sure to provide plenty of implements for scooping, carrying, and shaping.

- Don't forget all those free playthings in the backyard or park: pebbles, leaves, feathers, pieces of bark, mud, fluffy dandelions to blow away.

During this year of growing, climbing, swinging, running, building, stacking, stringing, scribbling, your Two-Year-Old is honing her skills. Every stumble and tumble is a learning experience that means fewer tumbles later. Every tower of blocks that falls will eventually lead to taller, more stable towers. Each time she fits a triangle into the triangle hole of the puzzle, or grasps a crayon, her abilities are strengthened.

And with each passing month, her body is growing more mature, more regulated, and more ready for all the adventures she will embark on when this year comes to an end.

TIME CAPSULES

These developmental signposts are general guidelines and should be kept in perspective. They are not a set of tasks that you must anxiously check off as your Two-Year-Old accomplishes them; rather, they indicate the stages of development most children experience during their third year of life. These are averages; few children do everything exactly according to this schedule.

Rather than using Time Capsules as a way of comparing your child to others, we suggest you use it as a kind of travel log—a way to anticipate what's coming up next, to know what to watch for so you don't miss any of the marvels of your child's year.

24 Months

Your Two-Year-Old is probably walking fairly skillfully now, but she may still watch where she puts her feet. She can stand on tiptoe and may be safe on stairs, but she still climbs with two feet to a step. She can throw and kick, but not accurately. She may climb out of her crib. She enjoys physical activity and sand and water play. She enjoys rhythm and sways to music. She has good wrist movement and can turn handles and lids. She can do a simple puzzle, although she may jam the pieces instead of trying to fit them. She can hold a crayon and scribble, turn the pages of a book one at a time, and make a tower of about six blocks.

30 Months

By midyear, your toddler continues to be more agile. She can stand on tiptoe and may be able to jump with both feet off the floor or balance briefly on one foot. She's better at moving through space: she can avoid obstacles, turn corners, change speed. She enjoys moving to music. She moves her kiddie car along with alternating feet, but she may have trouble with tricycle pedals. She may be able to climb stairs with alternating feet. Her fingers are more independent. She may be able to handle a brush and poster paints. She may manage a six-piece puzzle, and is learning to turn the pieces to fit. She enjoys folding paper and laundry.

36 Months

By year's end, she climbs well, may be able to pedal a tricycle, and is in general much stronger and more graceful than at the beginning of the year. She may have daytime bowel and bladder control. She can make vertical, horizontal, and circular strokes with a crayon, and may scribble and "draw" for as long as fifteen minutes. She fits puzzle pieces together by thinking about them, rather than through trial and error. She can build a tower of more than eight blocks.

QUESTIONS AND ANSWERS

Q: *My daughter has been walking for nearly a year, but she's quite clumsy. Whenever she runs in the house, she bumps into walls or furniture. Also, she drops things, especially when she's reaching for something else. Is this normal?*

A: Yes. It's normal to be clumsy, especially when running. And dropping things is common behavior. It's almost as if once your daughter sees the new object, she completely forgets about whatever she had in her hands.

Her coordination in both areas should improve this year. If she continues bumping into furniture, however, you might want to have her vision checked to make sure she can see the obstacles she needs to avoid.

Q: *My son, who is twenty-seven months old, is only in the fiftieth percentile in height, but in the ninetieth percentile in weight. He's chunky rather than fat. Our pediatrician says he is fine, but I'm wondering if I should do something to slim him down.*

A: Although much has been written about the negative effects of childhood obesity, it's important to remember that not all large children are fat children. If yours has inherited large bone structure or a muscular build, that will add to his weight even though he is not fat. Also, you might reassure yourself by checking his "sitting height." Are his legs relatively short, as part of his total height? If so, he may well lengthen out this year, which will bring his percentiles somewhat closer together.

Q: *My son, who is two and a half, loves to take all his clothes off. Often when he's not wearing clothes, he plays with his penis. I've tried to discourage him, but he persists. I'd rather he didn't do this. How can I get him to stop?*

A: Your Two-Year-Old is in the midst of the age of discovery, and one of the things he's discovered is his own body. He's been learning to point to and name his knee, his toes, his nose. If he is spending less time in diapers, he has more opportunity to learn about his genitals. Your best bet is to validate his interest in his own remarkable body, teach him the accurate names for his genitals (avoiding cute euphemisms), and gradually remind him that bigger boys usually keep their genitals covered and don't handle them in public. He'll soon get the idea that it's fine to have them and touch them, but there's a code of etiquette concerning private parts in our society.

Q: *I know Two-Year-Olds are famous for being physically active, but how can you tell the difference between normal activity and hyperactivity? My son is very active, fidgety, squirmy, and impulsive. I have read that these are symptoms of true hyperactivity. Is this true?*

A: Hyperactivity (more precisely, Attention Deficit Hyperactivity Disorder—ADHD) is usually pinpointed when children enter school and seem unable to handle the expectations of the classroom and schoolwork. In the case of active young children like your son, it's particularly difficult to sort normal behavior from hyperactivity. What Two-Year-Old isn't squirmy, impulsive, and energetic? As your son grows older, see how his behavior matches that of his peers. Can he participate in age-appropriate activities, or is he always veering off in his own direction? Can he sit (reasonably) still for a story with other children his own age, or is he the only one galloping around the room? If you see persistent evidence that he's at the extreme end of the continuum, you may want to have him evaluated.

Q: *My daughter just turned Two, and her grandparents gave her a tricycle for her birthday. She gets frustrated because she can't work the pedals. When will she be ready?*

A: Pedaling in a circular motion requires a level of coordination and strength that most Two-Year-Olds don't have, although many can manage by their Third birthday. In addition, a tricycle has to be steered more precisely than the riding toys your daughter is probably accustomed to. If she finds it frustrating, you might want to put the tricycle away for a few months, then ask her if she wants to try it again.

If she doesn't have the strength and skill to manage the tricycle, however, she probably won't have the ability to handle it safely, either. That's another reason to wait until later.

3

A Mind of His Own:
Intellectual Development

Your Two-Year-Old begins this year with a well-developed brain and a maturing capacity to think. All last year, as he galloped around the yard and fiddled with the plastic boats in his bath, he was learning about the physical world and how objects behaved. Now he is ready to build on that foundation, combining his observations and benefiting from his increased memory and ability to think symbolically.

"When Rasheed was eighteen months old," his mother recalls, "he liked to stand on a stool at the sink and pour his own water. He always filled the cup to the top, and of course it would spill when he picked it up. He always seemed surprised when it spilled, even though it always happened.

"Now that he's Two, if I pour his juice glass too full, he says, 'Too full, Mommy. Spill! Now he knows, in his mind, what's going to happen. He doesn't have to see it happen first. He's really streamlined his thinking."

Last year, your One-Year-Old collected observations

about his physical world—what heavy feels like, what fits and doesn't fit, what bends, what breaks, what tastes good. He mastered the law of gravity by endless experiments in which he dropped rocks, shoes, cups full of orange juice—and concluded that they always fell down, no matter how many times he repeated the experiment.

In addition, through his experiments, he began to understand object permanence—the sense that things have an independent existence, even if he can't see them.

Gradually, he applied that understanding to his loved ones, accepting that Mom and Dad were still around even if they said good-bye and drove off to work.

And he began to understand that he was separate from them, that he was an individual self who could influence other people and other objects. He began to tackle the concept of cause and effect.

By the time he turned Two, he was beginning to comprehend sequence—the idea that events follow one another in a predictable pattern. And he was beginning to understand the idea of quantity, as in "more juice," and some rudiments of time and space.

Now, at age Two, your child is about to begin a whole new intellectual phase. Like Rasheed, he will begin to apply his mind to his experiences in new ways.

Some Key Elements in Two-Year-Old Thinking

- He is developing abstract thinking. He can think about the attributes or behavior of an object or person in his mind, without actually observing the object. As this capacity develops, he begins to pretend for fun and to use pretense to get what wants. And he begins to use words that describe perception, not just real attributes: "It looks big," or "See, Mommy! Bear is happy!"

* He is developing memory. He has collected enough experience that he can now recall events in his mind.
* His understanding is reflected in speech and language, and he uses speech to help him think. The development of language and higher thought are intimately connected (for more on how this works, see Chapter 4). Emma, for example, talks herself to sleep every night. Her parents can hear her chatting softly to herself and to her doll about the events of the day. This typical Two-Year-Old soliloquy is a form of thinking out loud. Later, Emma will continue this stream of consciousness silently.
* His thinking is highly literal, because he lacks enough experience to allow for subtlety, abstraction, or the day-to-day complexities of life.

Lauren, nearly Three, is riding in the car with her father. "What's that sign, Daddy?"

"It says 'Do Not Pass,' honey."

"But you passed it, Daddy!"

Thirty-two-month-old Adam is in a restaurant with his parents. The adults ask the waitress if they can share their meal with their toddler, rather than ordering for him. "Sure," she replies. "I'll bring him an empty plate."

At that point Adam, ordinarily a quiet, cooperative toddler, bursts into wails of grief at the image of everyone enjoying a hearty meal except him, with his sad, empty plate.

Rasheed, spotting a kite flying in the distance, is told

he has "sharp eyes." "No," he says, "My eyes are soft."

- Two-Year-Olds have difficulty distinguishing between animate and inanimate objects. Last year, you may have noticed that your One-Year-Old treated other children like pieces of furniture (or punching bags!). This year, you'll observe your Two-Year-Old treating furniture as though it's alive. "Bad chair!" he is likely to tell the chair that "tripped" him. Watching the fire burst from the embers in the fireplace, he may say, "The fire waked up!" If he sees clouds moving across the sky, he may assume they are living creatures moving of their own will.
- His understanding of cause and effect, along with his growing ability to reason and to remember, will help him accept limits and manage his own behavior.
- Your Two-Year-Old is voracious in his desire to acquire that experience. Last year, he pursued experience physically. That continues, but this year he will also seek experience by asking questions. He will want to know what the rabbit is eating, why that man has his arm in a sling, or where the sun went.

Now, he stands at the brink of true thought: all his equipment is in place and ready to go. He is about to initiate a circular process, a sort of feedback loop, in which his growing experience refines his thoughts, and his ever-refining thought process can be applied more effectively to new experiences. This is called learning, and it is a lifelong journey.

Let's break down some of these concepts and see how

they fit into his world, then go over some ways that you can help him.

NUMBER

Your toddler is unlikely to master arithmetic this year, but his concept of quantity is becoming clearer. He may hold up two fingers when asked his age; at first, he may be copying you, rather than mastering an arithmetic truth. But later in the year, it shows that he understands that there are different amounts of things. You'll hear him use more words that have to do with quantity around the middle of the year: He'll say "more" and "another." He may be able to say "one" and "two" this year, but he's unlikely to learn "three" until next year.

Two-Year-Olds usually have not mastered the idea of conservation of matter, or number. For example, in Jean Piaget's classic experiment, he showed two equal balls of clay to a child, then rolled one into a different shape. Very young children had difficulty accepting that the two shapes still contained the same quantity of clay that they did before. Similarly, your Two-Year-Old may think she's getting more juice if it's in a smaller glass that looks "full"—even if she watches you as you pour it from a larger glass to the smaller one.

How to Help

• Talk about quantity in the context of daily life. Say, "One cracker for Jeremy, one cracker for Daddy." Or,

"Jeremy, you made a big tower. It's bigger than the tower Daddy made."

- Have your Two-Year-Old help you prepare a recipe. Explain the amounts of things as you measure. Show him two eggs, one cup of flour, and so on. Don't expect him to master these quantities, at least early in the year. But after many experiences with real, tangible quantities, he will eventually absorb the words and the concepts effortlessly.

- It's fine to count things for your child, so he is exposed to the words for numbers. But don't try to teach him to count by rote this year. It's more important for him to connect number concepts with actual objects and quantities.

- Colored rods (such as the Cuisenaire rods often used in schools) that show relative "sizes" and relationships are enjoyable for the child to manipulate and provide a tactile, visual idea of number. It's important, at this age, that they be offered as a toy, not as a "lesson."

SPACE

By the time your child celebrates his Second birthday, he has mastered some basic concepts about his physical world. He has a grasp of object permanence, for example, and has learned through many experiments that small objects fit into large ones but big things do not fit into little ones. He learned that objects always fall in the same direction—down.

Now, at Two, he has learned some basic words about space: "here" and "there," for example. His supply of words that relate to space and location will increase rapidly this year, especially after midyear. At that point, he will become much more specific: he will say something is "far away"; if you ask him where the book is, he may reply, "Under the bed." He will also ask more "where?" questions, as he seeks to know where animals live, where things go, what's beyond the mountain.

TIME

It's not hard to see why last year your One-Year-Old might have had trouble grasping the idea of time and all the words, rules, and delays that go with it. After all, time is a highly abstract concept that a child cannot see, feel, taste, or climb.

Yet at age Two, children begin to absorb this elusive idea, bit by bit. Several elements are required:

- Experience. Living through days and weeks immersed in time gradually builds up memory of events, and their patterns and sequences.
- The ability to hold mental images in mind. The ice-cream cone or trip to the zoo that you promise "this afternoon" has to exist as a mental image even though your child has not yet experienced it.
- Memory. Your Two-Year-Old cannot absorb ideas about (or words for) the past until he is able to recall past events.
- Vocabulary. It is largely through their words that we can track the way Two-Year-Olds view the passage of time.

    For example, early in the year, the Two-Year-Old

may use the word "now" and show an understanding of things happening in the present. This is a continuation of the "here and now" world of the One-Year-Old. Later, he begins to show an awareness of the future, using words and phrases like "soon," "in a minute," and "after." He may show some understanding of sequence, saying, "first we wash hands, then we have snack."

During the second half of the year, words relating to time become more numerous and more specific. As the child nears the age of Three, a clearer sense of the past become evident through language. However, it will take longer for a child to be precise. Many will be like one little girl who uses "Saturday" to describe anything that happened in the past. Ever since her mother reminded her, "Remember, Brianna? We were there Saturday," she has seized on that one word and applied it to any past event.

How to Help

- Early this year, talk about sequence, rather than rigid time words. For example, a comment like "We'll go to the park after Daddy gets home" reinforces the idea that events follow one another. If you limit your time conversations to "We'll go to the park at three o'clock," your words won't sink in.
- Don't try to "teach" the more complex time words, such as "Yesterday" and "next week." You can use these words, but don't expect your child to absorb the concept until later, probably when he's Three.
- Incorporate discussions about sequence, speed, and du-

ration into your conversations. Continue to call your Two-Year-Old's attention to events and things— turtles that walk slow, birds that fly fast, whether his socks go on before his shoes or after his shoes.

- Ask "Remember?" questions. "Remember when we were in this store and all the lights went out?" "Remember the orange butterfly Uncle Tony caught by this bush?" Your Two-Year-Old doesn't need to be able to respond to these questions to enjoy and think about them. As his language abilities improve, however, he will respond—and probably remind you of some details you forgot.

I CAUSE, THEREFORE I AM

One of Seth's favorite toys is a Sesame Street telephone that lets him converse with Big Bird or Ernie if he "dials" the right number. Last year, he would take the telephone to his mother and say, "Talk Ernie, Mommy." Shortly after his Second birthday, it dawned on him that he could cause these wonderful sounds to happen if he performed the correct actions. Now he understands that he has to push the number buttons in just the right way, and he's getting better at it every day.

Throughout this year, Seth will develop a clearer idea of himself as someone who can cause things to happen, and he'll refine his ability to sort out plausible outcomes (such as reaching Ernie on his toy telephone) from less plausible ones (like causing the rain to stop by yelling at it). This ability, along with his capacity to anticipate, will make it easier for him to manage his own behavior by year's end.

How to Help

- Talk with your Two-Year-Old about his activities in ways that emphasize outcomes: "I see you drank all your juice. Now it's all gone," or, "You made this tower tall. What will happen if you put a big block on top?"
- Talk about causation in your own daily life. "I left the ice cream out and it melted," or, "If we put more seeds in the bird feeder, the birds will come back."
- Ask him to anticipate outcomes, either in stories or in real life. "What do you think will happen when Goldilocks sits in Baby Bear's chair?" or "See that man on the ladder? He's sawing a branch. What do think will happen when he's finished sawing?"

CLASSIFICATION

At Two, your child is beginning to develop an understanding of categories and groupings of objects by a certain attribute: For example, he is able to pick out all the red blocks, or point to all the dogs in a book about animals.

But this year, his ability to refine and sort will grow dramatically. For example, he realizes that he can sort a group of objects in a variety of ways. He can select just blocks, because they are square, or just balls, because they are round. But when he makes a collection of red objects, he has to include some blocks and some balls. Later, he will sort girl dolls from boy dolls, and he'll arrange all the trucks in order, from smallest to largest.

As a One-Year-Old, your child probably classified physically, by making piles of objects. This year, he'll begin to do some of that sorting and rearranging mentally—instead of with his hands and eyes. So this year, not only is his classification system growing ever more sophisticated, it is becoming an intellectual ability rather than a physical-sensory one.

Something else happens to sorting behavior this year. Matthew always enjoyed picking the trucks and cars out of any assemblage of toys and piling them and lining them up. Now, shortly after turning Two, Matthew has begun lining the cars up on a roadway that he has constructed of long, flat blocks. He is chugging the cars along the road, and has discovered how much fun it is to crash them into one another. As the year goes by, he will incorporate more elaborate scenarios into his car-crash drama, with red cars crashing into silver cars; he also will include lots of talk and characterization. What started out as sorting play has evolved into imaginative play.

IMAGINATION

As your child moves beyond the concrete, here-and-now world that occupied him as a One-Year-Old, a whole galaxy of experience is opening up within his own mind. His improving memory means he can call up experiences and observations from the past. This ability to imagine has great impact on his future ability to think creatively, to interact socially, and to handle his own feelings. This year, pretend and imaginative play is a form of practice for your child. Last year he repeated the same physical operations over and over; this year, he practices abstract operations—the way a Daddy carries a child, the way a fireman might squirt water on a fire. In this way, he "masters" ideas of social interaction.

Piaget believed that imagination in a young child is closely tied to cognitive ability, and becomes incorporated into intelligence as the child grows older. Thus, an imaginative Two-Year-Old who combines his toys in unorthodox ways and creates a new game out of them will eventually put ideas and information together in unorthodox ways. A child who plays imaginatively as a toddler will be a more flexible thinker as an adult.

Kyle's favorite toy is his child-size kitchen, with sink, stove, and utensils. He loves to bustle around, imitating the way his parents work in the real kitchen. Sometimes he serves his mother "spaghetti," and other times he lines up his stuffed animals and plays a rather strong-minded chef, announcing in no uncertain terms what each animal will have for lunch.

Imaginative play often grows out of sorting play, as it does with Matthew and his cars. Over time, it also seems to extend naturally from imitative play. First, Melissa imitates Mommy by carrying a purse over her shoulder. Later, she carries the purse, looks for her car keys, and "buckles" a doll into her wagon. Soon she's playing the role of Mommy in a whole series of errands and adventures.

In other kinds of creative play, a Two-Year-Old practices extending his understanding into absurdities and humor. Andrea, who is nearly Three, is helping her mother snap green beans in a bowl. On her own, Andrea takes a bean and dabs it behind her ears, then her mother's ears, like perfume. Then she squeals with laughter. Andrea is not merely imitating, the way she did last year; she is being deliberately silly: Eau de Green Bean! How droll!

How to Help

- Respond positively to your Two-Year-Old's creativity, appreciating what he tells you, enjoying the "spaghetti" he prepared for you.
- Don't expect him to make a clear distinction between fantasy and reality this year. But you can help him begin the process by using words like "real" and "pretend." You can say, "Thank you, honey. That 'chocolate milk' was delicious. It was so good, I'm going to go get some real coffee."
- Read, read, read. (See Chapter 4 for suggestions of suitable books for Twos.)
- Be mindful of your child's exposure to television and movies. While these amusements can expand her universe, they can, especially if poorly selected, replace the development of her own imagination with a studio's imagination.
- Ask your Two-Year-Old to tell you a story. His response may be brief and somewhat disjointed, but you should appreciate his efforts.
- Provide props for dress-up and role-playing. Hats and headgear are ideal: they are visible symbols of different roles (cowboy, firefighter, queen), and take just seconds to change—an attribute that suits Two-Year-Old attention spans.

- Provide things to carry other things in, such as old purses, lunch boxes, and backpacks.
- Make a mirror available so he can see himself in all these roles. Full-length is best; mirrors in the child's play area should be unbreakable.
- Within the limits of safety, give your child access to household items that aren't officially toys so she can select her own props. A Two-Year-Old can create an entire Cecil B. DeMille production with flat cans of cat food, several glasses cases (without the glasses), green peppers, and business cards.

HUMOR

By the end of last year, your child was beginning to develop the foundations of an appreciation of humor. He found great amusement in falling down on purpose or bumping into things. And he enjoyed the absurd or incongruent, like you wearing a fuzzy slipper on your head.

And this year, while the slapstick element continues, your child's sense of humor will reflect his growing intellectual abilities. More and more, his expressions of delight will relate to things that don't quite fit, like the slipper hat or Molly's green bean perfume. Any silly question or deliberate mistake by an adult is likely to generate amusement, whether you say, "Is this Michael's elbow?" as you point to his eyebrow, or simply try to put the wrong piece into a puzzle.

As his vocabulary and language skills grow, your Two-Year-Old will begin to enjoy verbal humor. But he will prefer silliness to subtle irony this year; funny songs and silly rhymes will delight him.

GAMES AND TOYS THAT STIMULATE THINKING

To a great extent, any toy that's capable of keeping your child happily occupied is probably a good one for stimulating her cognitive abilities. Here are some good choices.

- Toys that can be used as props for pretend play. Toy brooms, dustpans, hammers, and saws are appropriate for a broad age range, because they can be used for simple imitation earlier, then as props for more imaginative games later on. These toys should be simple and realistic, allowing the child to embellish them in his imagination.
- Puzzles and shape sorters. Three or four shapes are about all most Two-Year-Olds can handle.
- Stacking and sorting toys. The same ones he played with last year are probably still fine, because he'll find entirely new ways to use them.
- Empty boxes (check for sharp staples) in assorted sizes. Big boxes can be anything from vehicles to houses to jails; smaller ones can be stacked and arranged as construction blocks, zoomed around as doll vehicles, or used to sort and classify other toys.
- Activity boards (doors that open, telephone dials, hinges, etc.).
- Picture lotto and memory games.
- Containers of different sizes, and something to fill them with (like water or sand) help your Two-Year-

Old grasp the idea of quantity, bigger and smaller, empty and full, partly full.
• Singing and word games that involve repetition reinforce your Two-Year-Old's sense of sequence, time, and anticipation.

WHAT ABOUT GIFTEDNESS?

It's hard to watch a Two-Year-Old's mind unfold and not think he is absolutely brilliant. His ability to learn and think are amazing indeed.

But even if your child does turn out to be quite the genius, chances are you won't have any definitive answers for another few years. Standard IQ tests aren't considered accurate until after age Three, so it doesn't make sense to seek a formal evaluation of your Two-Year-Old.

No matter how bright, most healthy, normal Two-Year-Olds need pretty much the same opportunities for intellectual development. There will be plenty of time later for special programs and lessons; this year, your Two-Year-Old needs a warm, responsive environment and plenty of opportunity to stretch his mind and imagination.

TIME CAPSULES
24 Months

The just-Two-Year-Old's ability to remember and to recall earlier events is growing. He has a clear understanding of the present, and may use "now" words appropriately. He is beginning to understand the concept of future, as evidenced in his use of time words like "soon" and "gonna." He will begins to use many more space words between now and midyear to describe where things are and where he's going. He has trouble distinguishing between animate and inanimate objects.

30 Months

Now his use of time words increase dramatically and become more specific. He may use words to describe the past ("last night," "morning," etc). He may understand the number 2. His use of language suggests he take things very literally. His fantasy and pretend play increase. Soon, he will begin to use past tense, though not always accurately ("I goed," "Daddy eated it up.")

36 Months

Toward his Third birthday, your child's memory has improved, as has his ability to concentrate. He may begin to talk about the past and use past tense. He may be able to understand the number 3, and may be able to "count" beyond that—but it's likely to be rote repetition rather than numerical understanding. He can match some colors. He can distinguish between an open figure (a squiggle drawn on a page) and a closed figure (a circle). He may be able to remember three directions at a time. His imagination is blossoming, as is his ability to talk about what he's thinking. His sense of humor inclines away from slapstick and toward incongruence and verbal silliness.

QUESTIONS AND ANSWERS

Q: *My son and daughter-in-law allow their children to watch a lot of television. I'm concerned about the effect that might have on the intelligence of our grandson, who is two and a half and really a bright little boy. Do you think too much television affects a child's intelligence?*

A: The role of television in the lives of children certainly has a bad reputation, and there is some reason for this. For too many children, it becomes a substitute for social interaction and creative activity. Yet television, used and controlled carefully by the parents, can be an enriching experience for toddlers. For that to be the case, however, parents need to select programs with care and limit the time spent viewing. Most experts recommend that very young children view no more than an hour of television a day.

Q: *I read recently that it's possible to teach children age Two and younger how to read, do advanced math, and learn foreign languages. Not only is this supposed to be possible, it's supposed to be good, because once they reach Three, their ability to learn has declined. If this is the case, shouldn't I be working with my son on letters and numbers?*

A: It's certainly true that children's ability to absorb new information is high during these early years. However, bear in mind that your Two-Year-Old is already learning an enormous amount of information, even if you aren't consciously "teaching" him. He is naturally curious, and is collecting hundreds of bits of information about his world, just through his own senses, his play, and his ordinary conversations with you.

Of course, letters, numbers and "facts" are part of the world, too. Your child will see words on cereal boxes, traffic signs, and on the front of Dad's team sweatshirt. Letters are as much a part of our world as any natural object, and Two-Year-Olds often want to know about these interesting little squiggles. If your child shows an interest in letters and numbers, there's no reason to deny him. Just remember that the learning process should still be child-driven, not parent-driven. To teach in a pressured way runs the risk of taking away his zest for learning.

Q: *What about a child (just turning Three) who lives in a fantasy world? Is an active imagination always a good thing? When is this too much?*

A: There are adults who are uncomfortable with imagination, and believe children ought to focus on the sensible, practical here and now. And certainly, there's a lot to be said for getting children engaged in the real world. But Two is an age when this capacity to see beyond everyday things buds, and should be nurtured. Imagination fosters intellectual growth later on. Imaginative play helps children develop empathy and polish their social skills in a safe setting. It helps them work out emotional stresses and anxieties, again in a make-believe setting in which they feel protected from real consequences.

If, however, a Two-Year-Old is so drawn into his fantasy world that he never relates to others, or has lost all interest in the pleasures of the real world, then there would be cause for concern.

Q: *My daughter is two and a half and can already identify letters and numbers. She seems more advanced than other chidren her age. How can we tell if she is gifted? Should we have her tested?*

A: Formal intelligence testing for children under age Three is not very reliable or productive. Until then, you can observe her for other signs that are common in very bright children: early language development, unusually creative use of language, fascination with abstraction and symbolic thought, and intense concentration.

If you think your daughter is unusually intelligent, it's unlikely that she'll require any different treatment than you would ordinarily provide—assuming that you provide her with a loving, stimulating environment and lots of opportunity to explore and learn on her own.

4

A Way with Words:
Language Development

Hannah, who has just turned Two, is out for a walk with her mother. She is growing tired, and she turns toward her mother, stretches up her arms, and says, "Carry you."

Her mother laughs and says, "Hannah, you can't carry me. I'm too big!"

Hannah raises her voice. She wails, "Carry you! Carry you!"

Hannah, it turns out, has no intention of carrying her mother. She wants to be carried, but she has trouble communicating this message because she's stuck in a Two-Year-Old thicket of confusing grammar rules. After all, her mother says, "Shall I carry you?" when she's offering her daughter a lift. Hannah is struggling with the ideas of subject and object, and with pronouns that mean "Mommy" sometimes and "Me" other times, depending on when you say them. Like most Two-Year-Olds, Hannah has learned the rudiments of speech and can usually make herself understood, at least within her own family (she did get carried eventually). But the rules of English are daunting indeed, and perfect speech is a long way down the road.

Two-Year-Old speech is imperfect, according to adult standards, but its imperfections are so logical and intriguing that linguists eagerly tape-record toddler speech to gain an idea of how language is acquired. During this year, your child will make miraculous progress both in the amount of vocabulary she acquires, and in the way she masters the complexities of English grammar.

This is the year that your Two-Year-Old will join the English speaking world. Some children, of course, have been speaking in sentences before Two, but most will begin this year with simple one- or two-word sentences. Most will become adept conversationalists by their Third birthday.

Of all the miracles you'll observe during your child's early years, the acquisition of language is one of the most awe-inspiring. Certainly last year you experienced this miracle as she pointed to objects and connected sounds with them, then began to reproduce some of these sounds accurately. She learned that speech—even speech that she didn't fully understand—is important. She responded to emotion in adult speech—angry or affectionate tones, for example. Finally by the time she turned Two, she most likely could combine words into true (if short) sentences, was able to understand a great deal of what was said to her, and could make some of her wants known through speech.

But this year, your child will most likely master true speech, speech with which she can communicate not only with you, but with others outside her family as well. Typically, she will talk in short sentences of perhaps two or three words at just Two, and progress to perhaps five or six words by year's end. When you ask your just-Two-Year-Old who's sitting on the chair, she may say, "Bear on it!" By Three, she'll say, "Bear's on the chair, Mommy."

VARIABILITY

It's important to note that during this year, children develop language at very different rates. One may talk in adult cadences at twenty-four months, another may be taciturn and difficult to understand at thirty-six months. Yet both are perfectly normal, and the differences tend to even out during the preschool years. The reasons for this variation are not entirely clear. Here are some possible explanations:

- Genetics. Some aspects of language develop may have a biological base. The rate at which tongue, palate, and facial muscles mature varies, as does the rate of brain maturity. If you or your spouse developed speech early, for example, your child may be an early talker as well.
- Temperament. Some children are natural plungers, eager to leap into any new situation. Others are cautious and avoid risk, waiting to see the lay of the land before committing themselves. A generally daring child will probably produce more speech than a highly cautious child.
- Gender. On average, little girls develop language a bit earlier than little boys.
- Family structure. First-born children seem to speak earlier than subsequent children, possibly because so

much of their early language experience is with other adults—their parents. Younger siblings converse with their parents, too, but they also imitate the imperfect speech of their older brothers and sisters.

• Environmental stimulation. A home full of affection, toys, books, and general good cheer is likely to enhance the development of language, and the best stimulation of all is the opportunity for conversation between the child and a loving adult.

TALK, TALK, TALK!

This year, your child will expand her vocabulary enormously. If you are keeping count of the words she knows and dutifully noting down her every utterance in her baby book, this is the year you'll probably have to give it up. At the beginning of the year, vocabulary size varies greatly, from a few dozen words to several hundred. By year's end, many children have vocabularies of nine hundred words.

Often she will commit a new word to memory by repeating it, often in play situations, and often to herself as she falls asleep at night.

Most of her words will continue to be nouns and verbs, but she will add adjectives and pronouns, along with a few adverbs, like "fast," "hot," or "scary," and quite a few imperatives, like "Gimme!" and "Do it!"

The word "too" often appears early because it's so useful to describe any kind of excess, as in "too hot," "too big," or "too hard." Of course, it risks misinterpretation. One thirty-month-old asked his father to play with him, and the father said, "Maybe later, Patrick. I'm too tired right now." A few minutes later, Patrick came back and whispered, "Are you ONE tired, Daddy?"

PUTTING IT ALL TOGETHER

Children may vary greatly in the rate with which they acquire language and learn to speak, but they are remarkably similar in the order with which they acquire certain skills this year. Your child may start using the past tense at thirty-one months and articles at thirty-five, while your neighbor's child may do those things several months later. But chances are they will both use past tense before they use articles; it's almost as if each skill unfolds naturally from the one before.

Linguists who study language acquisition believe that the key marker of a child's grammatical development is not age but average sentence length—the number of words, roughly, that she uses in a sentence. As her grammar and word usage develop, she uses adjectives, pronouns, and past and future constructions to lengthen and refine her sentences.

During most of this year, your child will probably speak in "telegraphic" sentences. If she were sending a telegram and had to pay by the word, she would eliminate any words not necessary for meaning. Therefore, Two-Year-Olds generally try to get to the point, using nouns and verbs for the most part, and leaving out articles, tense, and inflection. She might say, "Daddy come home get ice cream," which is a telegraphic way of saying, "When Daddy gets home, we'll all go out for ice cream." "I show book" is a simplified way of saying, "I'm going to show Grandpa my wonderful new book."

Her earliest pronouns will be "my" and "mine" (and later "I"), probably because they reflect her interest in herself and her possessions. She waits a bit longer for "you," perhaps because she can order you around quite handily without it by saying, "Read train book." Third-person pronouns like "he," "she," and "they" will come much later.

Like Hannah, your Two-Year-Old may be confused about the proper use of pronouns, and she may also be confused about gender: She may say "her" instead of "him" for a while.

She'll probably refer to herself by name ("Molly do it!") at first, then say "I" by year's end.

HOW TO SPEAK "TWO-YEAR-OLD" LIKE A NATIVE

Your Two-Year-Old does not learn grammar by imitation. She hears you speak, and recasts your complicated grammar according to her own rules. These rules are wonderfully logical and regular, and avoid some of the inadequacies of English like irregular verbs. Why say "I thought" when "I thinked" is much more consistent?

Molly, for example, is learning possessive pronouns. She knows how to say "mine" (in fact, like most Two-Year-Olds, she's an expert). She is just beginning to say "his" and "hers."

"For a while, I tried to correct Molly when she said, " 'Bear hurt hisself!' " her mother said. "I'd say, 'Bear hurt HIMself.' She'd just ignore me. Then I realized that in a way, she was being very logical. After all, we don't say, MEself, or YOUself. Why should we say HIMself?''

Similarly, Luis says "It breaked" when the truck's wheels come off. He knows that you're supposed to add a "d" sound at the end of a verb to form the past, so he does it—even if the two consonants are difficult to pronounce. Later, when he learns the irregular verb form "broke," he may well say "broked" for a while.

It's hardly surprising that Two-Year-Olds have these troubles when you consider that the most common, everyday English verbs are irregular and have confusing past tense forms: come/came, go/went, break/broke, sit/sat. The only reliable way she can form a past is by adding "d." To make matters worse, many common verbs like "cut," "hit," or "hurt" stay the same in the present or past tense. These are likely to come out as "cutted," "hitted," or "hurted."

LITERALLY SPEAKING

Two-Year-Olds take comfort in the familiar and the consistent, and so their development of vocabulary and grammar can be quite rigid—and often rigidly incorrect.

Your child might come into the kitchen and say, "I wanna cookie." A few minutes later, when you're carrying her, she may say, "I wanna down."

And her speech can also be very literal, as she tries to capture the fascinating qualities of the world with limited understanding and language.

"It's raining!" says Andrea, looking out the window. "It's winding!"

Adam points to the mailman and says, "He delivers antelopes!"

When someone in Jared's family sneezes, everyone says, "Bless you." If Jared sneezes and nobody responds, he announces, "I just bless you'd!"

"Look, Mommy!" shouts Katherine, standing naked in her wading pool. "I'm all barefoot!"

Marissa is playing house with her older brother. Andrew hides in the playhouse and says, "There's nobody home." Marissa spots him and shouts, "There's yesbody home!"

LANGUAGE AND THOUGHT

Your Two-Year-Old is learning to think and learning to speak at the same time, and these two processes are woven together. She speaks to herself to order her world and line up her thoughts.

You can hear her accompany her activities with chatter, especially when she is playing quietly by herself, or getting ready to fall asleep. This "self-speech," as it's called, serves as a kind of drill, sometimes going over new vocabulary words, and sometimes practicing grammatical constructions.

She also will use speech to order and confirm her world, and explain—to herself, mostly—just what's going on around her.

Two-Year-Old Ryan comes across a play wallet belonging to an older child. He carries it around, always commenting on its use: "He keeps his money in it. He keeps his money in here." When he tires of carrying it, he drops the wallet. Later he spies it on the floor: He turns to the adult. "He keeps his money in there!" Ryan doesn't yet know the first thing about money, but for his own Two-Year-Old reasons, he's enthralled with this object and its use, its function. He has the idea that it somehow represents the complex yet fascinating world of older children and adults, and he practices that idea by talking about it.

Similarly, at twenty-eight months, Jonathan uses speech to establish his ideas of space, location, and the roles people play. Over and over he says, "Daddy at work, Rachel at school, Grandma has toys in the closet."

LANGUAGE AND OTHERS

In studying the way young children used language, Jean Piaget distinguished between what he called the egocentric and the social functions of language. The egocentric function is self-directed and is essentially thinking, like the self-speech mentioned above. The social aspect is directed toward others and has to do with sharing feelings and ideas, influencing, resisting, and other kinds of communication.

Early in the year, most of the Two-Year-Old's emphasis is on egocentric speech. She doesn't much care who she's talking to, or whether anyone is really following.

But as the year progresses, your child will gradually shift her emphasis, and more of her speech will be directed to others. At first, she'll speak mostly to her immediate family. By Three, however, she will probably be able to make herself understood by adults and children outside the family (although some patience may be required). This is a true milestone. She no longer needs Mom and Dad as interpreters and is ready to move out into the world of nursery school.

Some of the ways your child uses language to connect with other people this year are:

- To make requests and ask for information.
- To describe her feelings and observations.
- To initiate social exchanges with adults, and with other children.
- To understand your spoken request, and then either acquiesce or resist.
- To tease or to entertain.
- To influence. She will use words to beg, boss, argue, negotiate, and compromise.
- To manipulate or mislead. As her understanding of the distinction between what is real and what is pretend grows, she will attempt to use language to misdirect you. She will learn pretense, the idea that language does not necessarily have to model reality. She'll learn that it's sometimes possible to fool people with language, and that it might be a useful tool for staying out of trouble. This year, Two-Year-Old attempts to weasel out of trouble are pretty transparent.

Robert, for example, is playing with a One-Year-Old cousin who doesn't talk yet. The adults, in the next room, hear a howl from the younger child and rush in. The little girl's mother picks her up and comforts her quietly. Robert watches this scene intently, then walks over to the mother and asks, in a small, careful voice, "Did she say 'hit'?"

Of course Robert is too young to understand that he

has just incriminated himself. But he can't resist the temptation to find out whether he's home free or not.

LANGUAGE AS PLAY

Just as your child plays with blocks and toys, she plays with words and language. Just as her physical play refines and develops her physical and intellectual abilities, her verbal play enhances and enlarges her language ability.

Like all play, her verbal play is focused on the enjoyment of the process, rather than any outcome. Early in the year, she will accompany her play activities with simple speech: "Me Mommy. Go store. Come, baby, get yogurt." Later, she will use language to spin a world of make-believe and attempt to involve other children in that world: "Justin, you be the king."

And just as she loves to swing, dance, and move about physically, she will enjoy the pleasure of saying words in rhythmic ways, in songs or verses. Most Two-Year-Olds are receptive to poetry because they are able to appreciate rhyme and meter as enjoyable repetition.

When it comes to songs and poems, the sillier the merrier. Two-Year-Olds love silly songs they can contribute to, like the song in which an elephant sits on anybody the child can name ("Willoughby, Wallaby, Weisha, an elephant sat on Keisha. . . . '').

How to Help

• Be responsive to the content and intent of your Two-Year-Old's speech, rather than to its precision. Your child is eager to communicate with you, and to learn from you. Don't derail her by demanding accuracy.

- Encourage her to tell you about what she sees and what she's doing.
- Allow her ample opportunity for unstructured play. It's at times like these that she'll practice her language at her own pace.
- Be mindful about background sounds in your home. Television and radio can be useful for language development, but they should not be a constant presence, like wallpaper. If they are always on, it will be more difficult for your child to pay attention to your speech and her own. It also may confuse her about the emotional and social content of speech, since television talk does not invite a response.
- Read and sing poetry, songs, nonsense rhymes, and change them for effect: "The eensy-weensy spider went up the . . . Christmas Tree" (instead of water spout). . . .
- When your Two-Year-Old pronounces a word incorrectly, don't correct her. But find a tactful way to repeat the word correctly. If Molly shows you a picture in a book and says, "Look, alibator!" you can reply, "Yes, Molly, that's an alligator, all right."
- Don't insist on perfection in grammar. It grows organically, through practice and maturity. No amount of reward or punishment will make a twenty-seven-month-old speak like an adult.
- Talk to your child, and not just to give orders. Talk about things, about what you are doing together, and what you see together. Respond to her questions, but

also listen to her responses when you ask her a question.

- Read-aloud time promotes listening skills in your Two-Year-Old, but it can also help her with speech and even critical thinking if you occasionally stop the story and encourage her to respond to it. Say, ''Where did that bunny go?'' or, ''Do you think the little train can do it?''
- Provide a toy telephone for pretend conversations.
- Not all stories have to come from books. Make up a few of your own, or retell shortened versions of fairy tales.
- Ask her to tell you a story. If she needs a hint, ask if she'll tell you a story about a dog (or whatever). Don't expect much, but some Twos can spin a yarn of sorts.
- Read to your child.

READ ALOUD

Story time can be one of the most enjoyable activities you share with your Two-Year-Old. Most children of this age enjoy stories immensely, although their ability to sit still may vary. But probably even the most frisky toddler will be willing to sit on your lap, or cuddle next to you, for a few minutes. Many toddlers have a considerable appetite for books, especially at bedtime!

With every book you read to your child, you're reinforcing many valuable lessons. Emotional closeness, the way you enjoy snuggling up together, the sounds of words, the emotional intonation of words, the meanings of words that she can see from the pictures that accompany them. Frequent read-aloud sessions can contribute to the ease with which older children master reading, as they begin to "read" along with their favorite stories.

You may find that your Two-Year-Old's degree of interest in story time will vary during the year, or with her mood. At the beginning, picture books, alphabet books, or very simple story books will appeal most.

How to Help

• Hold your child on your lap, or at least next to you on a comfy couch, so she can see the pictures (and the words) as you read.

• Most Two-Year-Olds demand that you read the story just the right way, over and over. You're in trouble if you leave anything out.

• Especially early this year, she will be most interested in the pictures, secondarily in the story. Page through the book, talking about the pictures. By midyear, she will probably want to hear the words—and hear them the same every time. By year's end, she will show great interest in what's happening in the story.

• Early in the year, she will most enjoy stories about things she knows, or might know—animals, families, towns. Toward Three, she will show more interest in fanciful and funny stories.

• Your child may show distress at certain parts of a story. One child, for example, loved the story about the Gingerbread Boy, but refused to let his mother turn to the last page because that was where the fox ate the

Gingerbread Boy. She solved the problem by making up an alternate ending that didn't upset him.

- Whether you're reading a story, a nursery rhyme, or just singing a song, you'll find that Two-Year-Olds love a place where they can chime in. Yours may not be able to say "Not by the hair on my chinny-chin-chin," but she'll probably love to give it a try.
- Be responsive to your child's attention span. If she gets squirmy, put the book down until later.
- Just because Twos enjoy simple stories and pictures, it doesn't mean many won't enjoy stories that they don't entirely understand—as long as there is something that delights them. Often wonderfully rhythmic language will enthrall Twos, even if it's technically too complex for them. After all, most Dr. Seuss stories don't make a lot of sense, but they sound wonderful.
- Make sure books are available and accessible in your home. Don't restrict your child to expensive classics that only can be enjoyed when you're around. You may still want to provide either board books or inexpensive paperback books if your child still treats them roughly, but make sure some books are freely available to her—in her car seat, on her highchair tray, in baskets next to her toys.
- If possible, avoid anthologies or large, heavy collections. Little children seem more comfortable with fairly small, lightweight books.
- Don't discourage questions during the story.
- If your child demands a certain book and you have run out of patience reading it, try taping it and letting her listen to the tape while turning the pages herself.

Of course, this should supplement, not replace, the intimacy of story time.

BOOKS FOR TWOS

Here are some books that appeal to Two-Year-Olds.

- *Goodnight Moon*, by Margaret Wise Brown, Harper & Row, 1947. An all-time favorite, in which a bunny in striped pajamas says good night to all the familiar things in his big, green room.
- *Blueberries for Sal*, by Robert McCloskey, Viking, 1948. A mother and daughter gather blueberries and encounter a mother and baby bear doing the same thing.
- *Caps for Sale*, by Esphyr Slobodkina, Harper & Row, 1947. There's lots of repetition in this silly story about a peddlar, his many caps, and a gathering of naughty monkeys.
- *When You Were A Baby*, by Ann Jonas, Greenwillow, 1982. Tells of all the things a big Two-Year-Old couldn't do then and can now.
- *Whiskers and Rhymes*, by Arnold Lobel, Greenwillow, 1985. Clever nonsense rhymes, illustrated with funny cats.
- *Goodnight, Twinklegator*, by Kazuko Stone, Scholastic Inc., 1990. An alligator creates a twinkling friend by connecting stars. A wonderful bedtime book with a place for the child to repeat "shhhhhh!"
- *Applebet*, Clyde Watson, Farrar, Straus, Giroux, 1982. This rhythmic, beautifully illustrated alphabet book is all about taking apples to the fair.

- *Harold and the Purple Crayon*, by Crockett Johnson, Harper & Row, 1955. Harold uses his purple crayon to illustrate this story and draw himself into and out of all kinds of situations. The irony may be lost on Twos, but those who are starting to draw will love the pictures.
- *The Runaway Bunny*, by Margaret Wise Brown, Harper & Row, 1972. A bunny practices autonomy by talking about running away and being found.
- *If You Give a Mouse a Cookie*, by Laura Joffe Numeroff, Harper & Row, 1985. All about the consequences of giving a greedy mouse a cookie. A cumulative story that's fun for Twos to follow and anticipate.
- *The Snowy Day*, by Ezra Jack Keats, Viking, 1962. A little boy explores the snowy city streets where he lives. Simple, appealing pictures and a warm text.
- *The Napping House*, by Audrey Wood, Harcourt, 1984. Cumulative story about a cozy nap.
- *The Very Hungry Caterpillar*, by Eric Carle, Philomel, 1969. The caterpillar eats his way through the book on his way to becoming a butterfly.
- *Cars and Trucks and Things That Go*, Richard Scarry, Golden, 1974. The usual busy Scarry illustrations of transportation scenes.

VOICE AND ARTICULATION

This year, your child's voice will gradually grow less babyish and singsong, and more childlike. Her singing voice may develop some control, although she'll hardly have perfect pitch. She will most likely have trouble pronouncing certain sounds this year and next, and may well have trouble making herself clearly understood to outsiders.

Many Two-Year-Old pronunciation "problems" are not problems at all, but rather are steps along a developmental path. It's not easy to wrap your tongue around some of the sounds in English; it takes time and practice. Some children have more trouble with articulation than others, but articulation problems at Two are not cause for concern.

TIME CAPSULES
24 Months

At Two, children vary greatly in size of vocabulary, from a few dozen words to several hundred. Most children speak in sentences, although they are short (two or three words) and telegraphic. Most sentences are about familiar objects, people, and activities and focus on the present. Your child may still rely on nonverbal signals to aid communication (pointing, gestures, and sounds of complaint). Her understanding of your speech is greater than her ability to produce speech. She calls herself by own name. Most of her conversation is either with herself or with you, rather than with other children or strange adults. She asks mostly "what" and "where" questions, and uses prepositions like "on" and "in".

30 Months

At midyear, her vocabulary increases rapidly. Her sentences are about events or activities, either in the present or future. Her use of tense is not accurate. She talks more about time, and uses words that refer to time and sequence ("I'm gonna . . ." and "after" or "then"). She now issues commands, and may threaten or name-call, especially with peers. She resists you verbally. She uses "I," or soon will. Although she still verbalizes to herself during play, she talks more to others. She asks more questions than before, and includes "when" and "who" questions. She enjoys the story as much as the pictures in her books.

36 Months

As your child approaches Three, her vocabulary has expanded dramatically and you have probably lost count. Although vocabulary size still varies greatly, some children know nearly a thousand words by the time they turn Three. She loves rhymes, poems, nonsense words, and silly conversations. She is adept at verbal fantasy and pretend. Her grammar is more adult in style, although the structure is still simple. She can talk about the past, although her tense and word choice may show confusion (she may say "yesterday," but it might refer to last week). She asks "why" questions.

QUESTIONS AND ANSWERS

Q: *I realize that children learn to speak at different rates, and it's not good to compare. But what if something really is wrong? How can you tell the difference* *between a child who is just a late bloomer, and a child who needs special attention?*

A: If a child is not putting words together into sentences by age Three, and doesn't seem to understand what's said to her, it would be wise to consult a pediatrician and ask for a referral to a language specialist. When a child is developing normally otherwise and understands speech but just doesn't produce it much, then most likely she will catch up in the next year or so.

Q: *My daughter is a great talker, and she has a very large vocabulary. But she persists in mispronouncing words with "r," and she sounds like Elmer Fudd. My husband thinks it's cute, but I don't. What should we do?*

A: Many children don't master all the English consonant sounds until they are Seven, and trouble with consonants is very common among Two-Year-Olds. Among the most difficult are "r" sound that your daughter has trouble with; the "th" in "their," which usually comes out "d"; and the "zh" sound in "treasure," which comes out as a plain "z." Most kids do learn, over time, to make the sounds correctly without specific teaching from adults. You can help her this year by enunciating as clearly as you can, but otherwise ignoring her pronunciation difficulties. And although her speech may sound charming to your husband, it might be helpful if he could downplay that reaction. Remarking, even favorably, on your daughter's speech may either encourage her to prolong this speech pattern, or make her self-conscious about her speech.

Q: *A friend gave our son a beautiful volume of fairy tales for his second birthday. I'd really like him to appreciate some of these classic stories and the wonderful* *illustrations, but he refuses to listen when I try to read them aloud. I've heard the same thing from other parents who would like their children to enjoy classic and good-quality literature rather than comic books. Why don't our children like these books?*

A: There are indeed some beautifully illustrated classics available for children, but few of them are really geared to very young children. Some, in fact, seem to be aimed at adults entirely. The pictures, although rich, are often too sophisticated for Two-Year-Olds to appreciate, and the stories are baffling because they are too complicated or use old-fashioned language.

For real-life reading aloud, you'd be better off getting some very simple fairy tales retold in picture book form (Paul Galdone has written quite a few good ones). But if you'd like to use your beautiful fairy tale volume, read the stories to yourself and then tell them to your child in simplified form.

Q: *We've always worked with our children to help them develop language, and we try to encourage them to speak clearly. Now our youngest, who is nearly Three and spoke very clearly just a few months ago, is beginning to stutter. When he does, we tell him to slow down and try again, but it doesn't seem to help. What can we do?*

A: When a child who has been speaking quite clearly begins to stutter between Two and Four, it's called developmental stuttering, and is probably no cause for concern. Most of the time, it happens when a child is trying a bit too hard to get his words out and gets stuck. It often cures itself in a few months.

Your son's stuttering will ease more quickly, however, if you can stand back a bit and try to generate an atmosphere of low-pressure calm in your home. When you ask him to start over, it increases his tension, and makes it even harder to get the words out. Your best bet is to take your time, listen to him patiently when he speaks, and concentrate on his message, rather than how smoothly he says it.

5

Caring and Sharing:
Social Development

This year marks the beginning of your child's life as a truly social being. This change will not take place overnight, but it will evolve. By year's end, you will share your life with a Three-Year-Old who relates to other adults with some confidence, holds his own in family interactions, and is actually learning how to get along with other children his own age.

At the beginning of the year, however, his One-Year-Old habits will persist. Your Two-Year-Old still views the world egocentrically—that is, he has not made the distinction between the way he views the world and how others view it. When he's talking to Grandma on the telephone, he may answer her question by nodding his head, not realizing that she can't see him nod. He will cling to hearth and home and find it difficult to separate from you. He is still testing the dimensions of his own autonomy, and will alternate between clinging to you and pushing you away. He will probably play alongside other children, but not really with them.

Then, toward the middle of the year, his interest in

other people will increase but his ability to handle himself in social situations will lag far behind his interest. Finally, by the time he turns Three, he will have learned a great deal about how to act, how to approach other people, even how to take turns.

Throughout the year, your child's growing intellectual and verbal skills will strengthen his social abilities. He will learn to approach other people with words, rather than just with his body. His growing sense of humor will provide him with a new tool for engaging family and friends in play. And his budding ability to anticipate events and control his behavior will serve him well.

One mother, whose son had been a notorious toy-grabber, recalls watching him play with a group of friends one afternoon.

"Cody was getting to understand the idea of taking turns. We had a rule in play group that you can have the scooter as long as you're actually riding it. But the minute you get off, someone else gets a turn. We always had to remind the kids about this rule.

"This time, Brittany was riding the scooter, and I could see Cody make a dash for it. And suddenly, he stopped short, like his feet were nailed to the floor. He had remembered the rule! Then he shadowed Brittany until she finally got off, and then he got his turn. I was so proud of him!"

Like Cody, your Two-Year-Old will make great strides in all his social skills this year.

Let's take a look at how your child's relationship with others will unfold this year, and how you can help the process along.

PARENTS. Your Two-Year-Old loves you best of all, and this adoration will continue this year. Early in the year, he'll relate to you more than to other adults or to other children. But as the year progresses, he will grow more interested and involved with people outside his family.

He will probably show great affection for his father, and relate to his mother and father in different ways. Colin, for instance, has decided that Daddy is for fun, and Mommy is for comfort.

"When I come home from work first," says his mother, "Colin says, 'Where's Daddy?' When my husband comes home first, Colin doesn't say, 'Where's Mommy?' He just runs over to him."

Still, she says, "When he wakes up in the middle of the night, it's me he asks for."

Your Two-Year-old is aware that human beings come in two styles—male and female—and is beginning to figure out differences between men and women. One mother, whose son usually sees her wearing jeans and sweatshirts, recalls getting dressed up in a flowery summer dress. Her Two-Year-Old looked at her in amazement and said, "Mommy! You look like a lady!"

Most Two-Year-Olds like nothing better than to help Mommy and Daddy. They love to participate in household activities, especially "helping" clean, prepare food, put away groceries, and such. Intrusive as this "help" can be at times, it's definitely best to encourage it. If you enlist your child's cheerful cooperation, it will pay off later not just in his willingness to do things for himself, but in his social and emotional foundation.

SIBLINGS. If your Two-Year-Old has older siblings, he will consider himself fortunate indeed. Hero worship gets going in earnest! Your younger child will probably hound and shadow an older sibling until he wears out his welcome.

If he acquires a younger sibling this year, your Two-Year-Old may not accept the newcomer well at first. Or, if he has a fairly unobtrusive baby sibling who suddenly starts to walk this year, he will find much cause for complaint as the little one gets into his things and disrupts his play.

Although your Two-Year-Old may annoy his older sibling this year, he can be a better companion now than he was at One. For one thing, he is a better playmate, having acquired language and an appreciation for imitative, pretend, and fantasy play. And second, he can respect other people's possessions and even follow some rules in play situations. Indeed, a friendly, playful older sibling can be an excellent teacher of social skills.

How to Help

- Protect your older child's rights. He needs his own age-level friends and games some of the time. He'll be less likely to resent your Two-Year-Old if he doesn't have to include him all the time.
- The same holds true for the older's child's privacy and his possessions. Until your Two-Year-Old learns to leave other people's things alone, make sure your older children have an off-limits place for their treasures.
- Protect your Two-Year-Old from being taken advan-

tage of by excessive teasing or general mayhem on the part of older children.

- Permit expressions of anger and bad feelings toward a sibling, but not violent or hurtful behavior. Encourage your Two-Year-Old to use words to say what's bothering him.
- If you have another child this year, prepare your Two-Year-Old for the event (see Chapter 6 for more on adjusting to a new baby).

PEERS. Derek participates in a small neighborhood play group, consisting of three Two-Year-Olds. The children have been playing together for about a year, and now Derek's mother is beginning to pine for the old days.

"It was easier last year," she says. "All I had to do was supply three of everything—I'd give them three pails, one per kid, and plop them in the sandbox. They'd play side by side, pretty much minding their own business. But now, each one wants all three pails!"

The hallmark of One-Year-Old sociability with peers is "parallel play." Young toddlers are primarily interested in their physical environment, and the properties of objects and toys; they appear to ignore other children (although they are learning a great deal silently). This tendency does continue into the third year, but Two-Year-Olds—especially at midyear—become much more involved in other children than they did last year.

The trouble is, they frequently lack the skills to approach other children, to defend themselves, or to handle the inevitable disputes. Young Twos may approach another child with an enthusiastic hug that knocks the victim down. Or they will hit or shove, then be completely shocked and appalled when the other child hits back.

Shortly after Derek's birthday, he began to take a greater interest in what his peers were doing. Soon, instead of just watching the other two play, he began participating—usually by grabbing or pushing.

"He never seemed to mean to hurt Michael or Sarah," Derek's mother reports, "but if he wanted something they had, he just took it. Michael would just sit there, looking sort of confused, and let Derek walk all over him. Sarah would grab it back.

"But now, Michael is more aggressive and they all pile on whenever there's trouble," she said with a sigh.

At midyear, it's not unusual for Two-Year-Olds to squabble and get into pushing and grabbing battles with their peers. Often, the trigger is a toy or possession.

At the same time, many Twos are becoming more adept at communicating. This development is not always pleasing to parents, since along with speech comes bossiness. But it also brings some relief to the violent excesses of the previous months. "Gimme that!" isn't gracious, but it's a step up from grabbing.

Language is now available for initiating an encounter that might earlier have begun with a grab or a push; pretend and fantasy now become incorporated into play in ways that foster cooperation. ("I'm the princess, you're the king . . . ").

Of course, there's still a long road ahead when it comes to playing "nicely" with peers. But most Two-Year-Olds are taking those first, essential steps toward being social creatures.

How to Help

- Don't expect social graces at this stage, but do teach.
- Play group experiences are valuable, even if children don't seem to get along too well.
- Don't be offended if other children aren't "nice" to your child. Your Two-Year-Old's peers haven't learned such an abstract concept.
- Do teach your child words for feelings ("hurt," "sad," "mad,"), and teach him that other children have the same feelings.
- Groups of Two-Year-Olds need adult supervision and occasional intervention.
- Even as you remain in the wings, ready to intervene when necessary, do permit some unstructured group play among Twos. Just as they need to have free time on the swings and climbing equipment, they also need to have unstructured opportunity to try out their social skills.

OTHER ADULTS. Last year, your One-Year-Old may have experienced bouts of "stranger anxiety," during which he was frightened of unknown faces. This year, through experience, your Two-Year-Old is less disturbed when a new person enters the scene. But that doesn't mean he will be entirely comfortable with others, especially if you leave—baby-sitters and day-care providers, may not be welcomed enthusiastically at first.

One of your Two-Year-Old's major tasks this year is separating from you. It's a necessary step toward independence, like weaning or learning to walk. It works best when it's gradual, and when he can see the advantages. And positive experience with caregivers can help.

HOW PLAY HELPS YOUR CHILD GROW SOCIALLY

Throughout his early years, play will be the engine that drives your child's development. As we've discussed in earlier chapters, he develops physically, mentally, and linguistically as he plays with you, with others, and with appropriate toys.

Last year, he manipulated blocks, boxes, stuffed toys, mud and pine cones seemingly endlessly, and in the process mastered what he needed to know about the physical world. This year, he'll continue many of those activities (with refinements), but he will now "play" with social interactions. When he's alone, he'll make his animals and dolls and vehicle act out social exchanges.

When he gets together with other children, he will express emotions like aggression and affection, and practice social skills like politeness, negotiation, and cooperation.

Through play, children learn the foundations of generosity. They can learn that giving results in receiving, and they can learn that by sharing, everyone has access to more toys. And Two-Year-Olds learn, through play, that some activities, including imitation and imaginative games, are more fun with more participants.

That's one reason children need a chance to play with one another, and why some of that play should be fairly unstructured. Play is a voluntary activity that is not graded or judged, and provides the freedom to experiment. It offers a chance to try out a range of behaviors and sort out what works from what doesn't.

EMPATHY

This year, your Two-Year-Old will not be able to put himself in another's shoes. He'll be better able to treat others the way he wants to be treated, because he will master some rules of social interaction ("Take turns"; "Don't hit"). But his understanding of the feelings of other people will still be dim.

Rachel, for example, was among the more bellicose toddlers in her day-care class. She grabbed toys instead of requesting; she cried when she had to wait her turn, and she hit when angry.

One day, however, a new Two-Year-Old named Andrew joined the group. And he turned out to be at least as aggressive as Rachel. When Andrew grabbed Rachel's book, she looked stunned. When Andrew swatted Rachel for pushing him out of line, Rachel wailed as though she was the victim of an injustice never before experienced in human history.

During this year, with some guidance from her family and teachers (and an occasional reality-check from Andrew) Rachel will gradually make the connection between what she does to others and what others do to her. She'll begin to understand that the bad feeling she gets when someone hits her is the same feeling another child experiences when she hits him. It's a difficult lesson—one that many adults never learn—and it will take more than this year to learn it.

But Two-Year-Olds are ready to begin learning lessons of empathy. Even Rachel, for example, is aware of distress in another child, and sometimes shows discomfort (even if she herself caused the distress). You can build on this awareness with your own Two-Year-Old this year by labeling feelings and talking about them, and listening to him talk about what he feels.

This year, as last, you need to be patient. He will learn to behave with more consideration, but don't expect his caring behavior to come from within. You will have to impose guidelines from without: "No hitting. Hitting hurts."

How to Help

- Talk about feelings and help your Two-Year-Old learn "feeling" words (see Chapter 6 for more on this).
- Model caring behavior yourself. Let him see you caring about the feelings of others. "I'll bet James felt sad when his cat ran away," or "What a pretty picture you made! You must be proud!"
- Teach reasonable rules about consideration for others. He will be able to behave in a courteous way long before he internalizes a mature sense of empathy (see "Etiquette," below).

SHARE AND SHARE ALIKE

Sometime during this year, you will probably see an amazing change in your toddler. He will begin to show an actual interest in the rituals of cooperative play and social interaction. A child who had absolutely no idea that hitting other children hurt them begins to show restraint. He learns that if he hits, the victim might hit back. Or if he offers a toy, then the other may offer one back. Or if he waits his turn, he'll get one soon.

One of the earliest parts of sharing that Two-Year-Olds learn is to take turns. This is a skill that you need to teach, just as you teach your child colors and shapes: in playful, enjoyable settings, you teach the simple rules of games. Your child does not yet need to understand the philosophical aspects of sharing and taking turns; that will come later. But this year he can learn the mechanics, and as he does, he will gradually see how much more fun playtime and games are when everyone takes turns.

For example, simply climbing up the ladder of the sliding board, one at a time, reinforces this idea. Singing "Old MacDonald" and giving each child a chance to make the sound of an animal reinforces this idea.

The sharing of possessions is somewhat more difficult, because there's a tangible object to be relinquished. Two-Year-Olds are natural hoarders. And yet, especially toward the end of the year, they are capable of understanding that it is possible for more than one person to use an object (say, a wagon) sequentially, or that some things (a pizza) can be divided among everyone in such a way that everyone gets enough.

Family mealtimes are one setting where cooperative values like sharing can be taught along with other table manners. When you cut a casserole or a loaf of banana bread into fair shares, or scoop servings of potatoes from a common dish, you are teaching your Two-Year-Old that social rules mean that everyone will be provided for.

How to Help

- Do articulate and enforce rules about fair play and sharing. Your Two-Year-Old and playmates may not obey these rules right away; they will need to hear a rule spoken many times before they will be able to internalize it.
- Provide your child with opportunities for play with peers.
- Play taking turns games and sing taking turns songs.
- Avoid forced sharing. When Two-Year-Olds are forced to part with precious possessions before they understand the meaning of sharing, it encourages them to grip their possessions more tightly.
- Before a play date, allow your child to set aside certain treasured items that he does not want to share.
- Have your child designate a Sharing Toy—something he is willing to take along on a play date and permit his friend to play with. Gradually, he will learn that he always gets the Sharing Toy back. An added bonus is that presenting the toy to the host, may make that child feel more inclined to share with the guest.

TWO-YEAR-OLD ETIQUETTE

Jordan, who is almost Three, has learned recently that etiquette greases the wheels of life. He has learned that asking for something politely gets him further than demanding. So now, if he wants someone to read him a story, he asks very nicely and says, ''Pleasethankyou!''

Jordan has little understanding of what the words mean, but he knows they're magic.

Like Jordan, your Two-Year-Old is ready and able to learn some simple rules about etiquette, just as he's learning about colors, animals, and how to do puzzles. Just keep the rules in line with what he's capable of. Behavior that would be rude in a Six-Year-Old may be normal and innocent in a Two-Year-Old.

- Be specific. Don't tell your Two-Year-Old to "be nice," and leave it at that. Instead, tell him, "Please pass these crackers to Sarah so she can have some too." Or, "Grandma has lots of bags to carry. You can help by carrying this one."
- Do teach simple table manners. Your toddler can learn to ask for food to be passed instead of grabbing or screaming.
- Don't put too much emphasis on apologies. It's fine to teach him the proper words to say when he has wronged someone, but don't expect his words to come from the heart.
- Don't forget to mind your own manners. If you demonstrate courtesy as a matter of course, he'll learn it naturally. And don't limit your politeness to adults. Say "please" and "thank you" to him, and to other children as well.

OFF TO NURSERY SCHOOL

As toddlers approach their Third birthday, opportunities for traditional nursery school open up. If your Two-Year-Old has been in a group day-care setting, he'll be an old hand at the challenges of nursery school and, eventually, kindergarten. He'll know all about the routine of saying good-bye to Mom or Dad in the morning, and he'll be a veteran at group play and sharing the juice and crackers.

If your child has been home with a parent, or with an individual sitter, he will need your support if he has to make the adjustment to a day-care center or nursery school this year. Keep in mind that this adjustment has more to do with learning to trust another adult than learning to adjust to other children, at least at first. The most important element of your child's experience will be the adult caregivers, preferably one special caregiver. Your Two-Year-Old is used to mattering a great deal to one particular adult (or two). He won't be comfortable if the caregivers are a blur, turning over, treating him mechanically. He has to establish intimacy and trust.

Studies have suggested that toddlers in a day-care or nursery-school setting actually explore more and partici-pate more in games and activities if they have established a close attachment to a particular teacher.

How to Help

- Tell your Two-Year-Old ahead of time that he'll be going to a special place to play. Talk about the things he'll do while he's there.
- Visit the school or center so he can see it for himself. This visit also reassures him that the things you told him about were true: Yes, there's a big sandbox under a tree, just like Mommy said.
- Talk about his new adventure in a positive way. You

may have guilty feelings about going back to work and being away from him, but try to cast the new adventure in a cheerful light.

TIME CAPSULES
24 Months

Early in the year, the Two-Year-Old is becoming aware of himself as an individual, distinct from his parents, and ready to move away from them into a larger world. However, he is still a beginner when it comes to social skills. His favorite people are his parents, followed by older siblings (but he may resent a younger sibling). He'll begin to play a bit with other children, but still engage in the "parallel" play of last year. He may be aggressive, but the aggression is not intentionally hostile. Or he may be acquiescent and bewildered by the aggression of others. He is more aware of social expectations, but he is not yet able to meet them reliably. His sense of humor is still essentially physical. He may call other men "Daddy" and other women "Mommy" until he masters the words and concepts necessary to correctly label other adults and their roles.

30 Months

The child at two and a half is ready to reach out to others, accepting separation from his parents more easily and showing interest in other children. Within his family, he behaves in contradictory ways: He is eager to help with domestic routines, but he is contrary and bossy. His growing interest in peers is not matched by social skills. His play sessions may begin with shared imitation and some verbal exchanges but often deteriorate into grabbing and shouting matches. He may say "man" and "lady."

36 Months

As he nears his Third birthday, your child is on the brink of true sociability. He has a clearer understanding of himself and where he stands in relationship to others. He calls himself "I" and others "you." He is a bit less possessive about his toys, and is able to share to a degree. Squabbles with peers are somewhat diminished; he pushes and grabs less, but fights more with words, issuing commands and calling names. Likewise, he uses words more and physical actions less in other aspects of his relationships.

QUESTIONS AND ANSWERS

Q: *My daughter's play-group sessions always seem to end up in battles and squabbles, usually over toys. When the children are at my house, I usually try to end the fighting. My neighbor says it's better to let them work it out themselves. She doesn't do anything unless someone is actually getting hurt. Which approach is best with Two-Year-Olds?*

A: Your neighbor is partly right, in that the primary advantage of social opportunities for Two-Year-Olds is to provide ample practice for their social skills. Naturally, they'll learn most if their interactions are not entirely adult-driven. They need a chance to sink or swim on their own terms.

However, Two-Year-Olds do not yet have many social skills to practice. They need to learn what behavior is appropriate and what is not, and they need adults to teach them that. Your best bet is to strike a balance between the extremes of hovering and ignoring. Perhaps you can start by structuring their play session to minimize conflicts (a small number of children and enough toys and materials for all, for example). Then let them play pretty much on their own for awhile. Don't expect perfection, and give the children a bit of time to move past their own disputes. However, be observant, and do intervene if things get out of hand or if one child is frequently victimized and another is consistently aggressive.

Q: *My Two-and-a-Half-Year-Old daughter gets along fairly well with other children, but she really prefers playing alone. I'm not talking about parallel play; she actually separates herself. She will play with others if they are there, but soon retreats to her own room, or her own corner of the playroom. She doesn't seem to be shy, just not very social. Should I be concerned?*

A: Not necessarily. Your daughter may just be an independent sort. As long as she plays with others some of the time, she is probably developing appropriately. Remember, however, that social skills must be practiced, and if she entirely avoids the company of her peers, she may not acquire the skills she'll need later, or the sense of ease in being part of a group. It's fine to let her play happily by herself, but try to keep a balance. She does need peer play for the social, intellectual, emotional, and linguistic stimulation that other children can provide.

Q: *My son, who is thirty-months old, is developing a bad reputation in our neighborhood. He really is a very physical guy, and he tends to get pretty aggressive with other children. He pushes kids out of the way, and when he really wants a toy, he'll kick the child who has it. Some of the other parents won't let their children play with him. What can I do?*

A: Aggression is not at all uncommon among children your son's age. However, if it's interfering with his play opportunities because other parents and children see it as a problem, then you may need to increase your efforts to teach your son social skills. If you have ruled out physical or emotional problems that might make him behave unusually aggressively (see Chapter 2 and 6), try working with him on politeness. Teach him the magic words he needs to ask for things. Encourage him to wait his turn. Give him strategies for approaching another child, or a group of children, to initiate play. You can teach these skills with role-playing games, or with dolls or puppets that take on the role of a child approaching a group and trying different strategies. Finally, reinforce what you've taught him about feelings—that he has them and so do other children.

Then, your best bet is to try to reintroduce him to social exchanges in measured doses. Enlist one of the other parents and explain that you recognize the problem and are working on it. Arrange a short play date with one child and praise your son when he plays cooperatively. He may always be physical and assertive, but he can learn to behave.

Q: *When we go to the play area in our development, my daughter is picked on by the other children. If she walks up to a group of other Two-Year-Olds in the sandbox, for example, they push her away and yell at her. How can I get them to be nicer to her?*

A: Two-Year-Olds have very primitive social skills, which may explain why the other children aren't behaving graciously. They haven't yet learned how to say, "Please don't dig there; that's our fort." Your best bet is not to take it personally, and don't convey to your daughter that she's being victimized. Instead, see if you can strengthen her own social skills. Two-Year-Olds often need help in learning to approach another child and initiate play. Suggest that she use words, rather than actions: she can go up and ask the children what they're doing, and watch for a moment before joining in.

Remember, also, that other children aren't going to make the same allowances for a child that her parents make. A Two-Year-Old who is catered to excessively at home may have trouble figuring out how to behave in a less protected environment. She needs to get accustomed to the more egalitarian skills of the playground.

6

Sometimes I'm Up, Sometimes I'm Down: Emotional Development

For several nights shortly before she turned Three, Courtney would awaken screaming. Her parents were accustomed to the ordinary nighttime wakefulness of Two-Year-Olds, and they knew immediately that this was different. Each night, they would find her cowering in her crib, pointing to the wall and screaming "Teeth! Teeth!"

Each night, they turned on the light, explained that there were no teeth to worry about, and comforted her until she finally fell back to sleep. But on the third night, Courtney's father sat with her awhile in the darkened room and asked her about the teeth.

"Monster teeth, Daddy," she said sleepily, and pointed to the wall, where a Windsor chair, illuminated by her nightlight, had cast a barred shadow on her wall. To Courtney, they looked distressingly like the fierce fangs of a Tyrannosaurus that she had seen in a television commercial for a movie.

Fortunately, Courtney's fear was easy to diagnose and cure. Her parents explained that it was just a shadow. They moved the chair to a different position in the room, and from then on their nights were peaceful. Later, they talked a bit about television monsters and what's real and what's pretend.

Like Courtney, your Two-Year-Old will experience all her emotions, including fear, in more complex ways this year than last. Her fear will be more imaginative and you may have to deal with nightmares and dinosaur teeth. Her feelings of pride, joy, and affection will come into their own; her feelings of anger and jealousy will be fierce and intense.

This year, your child's emotions will be intensified by her growing ability to think, to remember, to reason, and to create imaginary images in her mind. But those same abilities make it easier for you to comfort her, and they'll arm her with a greater capacity to modify her own emotions, to battle her fears, and to talk her way through her own distress.

Most of all, language will be her—and your—fundamental tool in managing her powerful emotions. Some of her feelings are happy ones, and she will happily share them with you. Others are unpleasant, and you can comfort her with words when she's frightened or worried.

In this chapter, we'll examine the nature of the Two-Year-Old feelings and look at some of the emotional tasks that your child is working on this year. And we'll look behind the scenes at some of the most typical Two-Year-Old behavior: She will swing wildly from mood to mood. She will try to anchor herself with rigid, ritualistic behavior. And she will interpret her growing world in unrealistic, even magical ways.

TEMPERAMENT

As any parent of more than one child can attest, children have profoundly different personalities. Variation in mood, energy level, manageability, and sociability are remarkably persistent throughout people's lives. Chances are that by now you know your Two-Year-Old well.

Although psychologists have battled for years over whether personality is determined by genes (and thus is resistant to change) or by environment (and thus can be altered), most now agree that the truth lies somewhere in between. It seems likely that every child comes into the world with a certain genetic underpinning, but this predisposition interacts intimately with her environment to produce a unique individual.

Dr. Stella Chess and her colleagues, who studied a large group of children for the first ten years of their lives, concluded that a child's essential temperament remains consistent. From the earliest weeks of life, babies varied in terms of energy level, sensitivity, distractability, and tendency to be either outgoing or withdrawn. Shy, tentative babies retained those traits as they grew up. Boisterous, outgoing babies became energetic, social children.

According to this research, most babies have a temperament that could be described as "easy"—reasonably regular, happy, sunny infants who aren't too distressed by disruptions, and can be comforted easily when something does go wrong. A smaller group was described as "slow-to-warm-up"—inherently shy children who needed more time to adjust to new situations.

Finally, a small percentage of children were described as "difficult"—fretful, irritable, quick to react negatively, and difficult to soothe.

Most babies, of course, have some attributes of more than one group. No child is absolutely sunny and unflappable in all situations, and no normal child is so withdrawn that she can't be ever tempted into social experiences.

What's important about these categories, and all research on temperament, is not that we should all become passive fatalists about our shy or difficult children. These traits, despite their likely biological origins, are not written in stone. What's important to consider is that children can and do flourish, whatever their basic style. Your task as a parent is to recognize your child's style, become sensitive to it, and work with it as you support her emotional and social development.

EMOTIONAL MILESTONES

Some experts believe children need to reach a series of emotional milestones as they develop, just as they do in their physical development. As with creeping, standing alone and, finally, walking, children need to master a progression of emotional tasks. A child who misses a task or is unable to master it may suffer emotionally later.

Dr. Stanley Greenspan has designated six such milestones between birth and age Four that provide a useful way of looking at your child's blossoming emotional life. If your Two-Year-Old is reasonably well adjusted, she has probably sailed through the first four of these stages, which include:

1. Self-regulation (birth to about three months). The newborn needs to get comfortable with the world, and organize her own senses enough to be receptive to interesting sensations.
2. "Falling in Love" (about two to seven months). The baby becomes engaged with the world and its delights. Chief among these delights is you—your face, the sound of your voice, the comfortable way you make her feel.
3. Developing intentional communication (about three to ten months). Now her expressions of delight and love are intentional. She responds to your voice with chatter of her own, and reaches out for an object you offer. She tries to get your attention by cooing and smiling.
4. Organizing feelings into emotional behavior (about nine to eighteen months). Now she expresses love by hugging, anger by hitting. She imitates emotional and social behavior. She practices separation in games like peekaboo and hide-and-seek.

For most of this year, your toddler is likely to fall in the fifth stage, which extends from about eighteen months to about Three years. During this period, Greenspan says, children create emotional ideas, and put ideas and actions together. You'll probably observe this as your Two-Year-Old plays, and her imitative play evolves into pretend play. She gets angry at her doll, comforts it, takes it to the doctor for shots, soothes it with imaginary lollipops.

Your Two-Year-Old is becoming capable of naming and thinking about her feelings. She is beginning to incorporate her understanding of emotions into her play, and her pretend play moves beyond the purely imitative into the realm of fantasy and imagination.

Finally, from about age thirty months to age Four, your child will achieve the sixth emotional milestone: True emotional thinking, as the basis for an active imagination, and an ability to sort out reality from fantasy. During this period, children incorporate thought into their emotional behavior, and this makes it possible for them to regulate their emotions, consider alternatives and anticipate outcomes.

At thirty months, Lisa loved to reenact scenes from her day-care center, which usually involved trying to get her dolls (and any willing human participant) to take naps. Her imagination would easily veer away from strict reality; teddy bears and dinosaurs tended to get up from their naps, pile into a handy toy shopping cart, and take a trip to the beach.

Now, at Three, Lisa's pretend play, while just as imaginative, is more realistic. If she portrays her day-care activities, she creates a more likely script, and sticks closer to it. Her animals have to look at books, then have snack, and finally sing a song.

Your own Two-Year-Old may not follow Lisa's pattern of thoughtful play until well into next year. The ages at which children achieve these milestones vary, but most progress through the same sequence.

The Nature of Two-Year-Old Emotions
AFFECTION AND LOVE

Two-Year-Olds love Mom and Dad best of all. You are an object of adoration in your Two-Year-Old's mind, and for good reason. You are her source of comfort and support, and if last year she was on occasion aloof, this year she truly appreciates you.

Your child is eager to please you, and she is growing more accomplished at showing—and requesting—affection. She'll smile, hug, and kiss. Early in the year, she'll be so eager to earn your approval that she may actually do your bidding much of the time. She'll prize your attention and your company, and she'll be eager to help you put groceries away, fold laundry, or fetch you a snack.

Toward the middle of the year, however, you may see more resistance and negative behavior. She will resist requests that she complied with a few months earlier. She will disobey you in a way that you know is deliberate, and seems designed to get your goat. "She knows how to push my buttons now," grumbles one mother of a thirty-two-month-old who seemed so delightful and uncomplicated six months earlier.

Even in her worst "Terrible Two" moments, however, she still needs your absolute love. You don't need to love what she did to the wallpaper with her new set of crayons, of course, but later, after you've dealt with her unacceptable behavior, you need to remember that she still needs physical affection and words of love from you.

How to Help

- Use words to describe your feelings of affection. "You're so nice to be with today." "Aren't you sweet to bring me a glass of water on this hot day!"
- Give your Two-Year-Old lots of physical and spoken affection even on those days when her behavior hasn't been ideal. You may not feel like hugging her while she's screaming in the supermarket, but don't forget to give her a loving good night later.
- Do continue to give hugs and kisses and affectionate words to sons as well as daughters. Little boys need parental cuddles just as much as little girls do, and they thrive on the affection of Dads as well as Moms.

ATTACHMENT AND AUTONOMY

One of your Two-Year-Old's major emotional tasks this year is to continue the long process of becoming a separate individual, aware of her own selfhood, and willing to venture out into the world on her own.

At Two, your child already has made great strides along this road. If you and she have established a warm, trusting relationship, she is learning that you are emotionally available to her even when you're not physically present. She's able to keep a vivid picture of you in her mind, and if she starts to miss you, she can comfort herself with your image—just as you derive pleasure from her portrait on your office desk.

By year's end, she should be able to part from you

more easily than before, whether she's starting nursery school, going to play at a friend's house, or staying with a sitter when you go out in the evening.

Some time this year, you may see a heightening of resistance and protest, a general contrariness that wasn't there a few months earlier. "I do it!" is a common refrain.

Jason, for example, insists that he can put on and tie his own sneakers, which is simply not the case. He refuses to let his mother put them on during the usual dressing routine. She has to allow extra time for Jason to demand, struggle, get the shoes on the wrong foot, and get his fingers tangled in the shoelaces.

At first, Jason's mother tried to force the issue. She insisted on doing it herself, resorting to bribes and threats just so she could get him dressed and out the door in the morning. Eventually, however, she realized that he was ready to try things on his own. Rather than fight him, she simplified the task by buying sneakers with Velcro closures, setting the shoes in front of him in the right positions, and letting him try. If he still got stuck and frustrated, she would say, "You did a great job. You did most of it yourself!"

Jason's mother wisely chose to accept Two-Year-Old (especially Two-and-a-Half-Year-Old) stubbornness and try to work with it, because it is a sign of developmental health. It means that a child wants to grow up, and is struggling toward that goal.

There are other signs of blossoming autonomy that you may see in your Two-Year-Old:

• Hoarding. Especially at the beginning of this year, your Two-Year-Old may signal her selfhood through possessions, or at least objects that she claims to possess. Some time before her second birthday, you probably began to hear the cry of ''Mine!'' resound through the house, especially when she was playing with other children. This year, she collects objects— books, dolls, hats, whatever, and derives a sense of power from being a possessor.

- Contrariness. Later in the year, she may try your patience by doing the opposite of what you ask or demanding the opposite of what you offer. If Dad is putting her to bed, she wants Mom. If you serve her favorite macaroni and cheese, she wants wants a peanut butter sandwich.

- Verbal resistance. Last year, and early this year, your Two-Year-Old signaled her resistance by squirming out of your grasp, running away, pushing away a spoonful of food with her hand. This year, she will still use her body to resist, but she will also begin to tell you with words that she doesn't approve of something. By year's end, you'll hear ''No! I do it!'' or ''I don't want carrots.'' Along with verbal refusals will come commands and orders; at times your little angel may seem more like a drill sergeant.

- Rigidity. Alyssa takes the same route from the back door, through the kitchen, around the dining room table, and up the stairs every time she goes up to her room. Anthony will not accept any liquid refreshment if it isn't served in his Spiderman cup.

The Two-Year-Old's growing awareness of the complexities of the world inspires a need for predictability and sameness, especially around the midyear. She feels safer when certain things remain the same, especially things that she can control. We'll discuss her love of ritual more in Chapter 8.

How to Help

- Allow your child to try new things, including things that may be a bit difficult for her. As long as she isn't overwhelmed by tasks that are beyond her, she will benefit from trying to pedal a tricycle or climb higher on the jungle gym.
- Don't come down too hard on contrariness and resistance. If she grumbles about a restriction but does what you ask anyway, that's good enough.
- Allow her independence to unfold gradually. Don't push her; if you do, she may be more anxious about leaving your side.

ANGER

Much of what prompts Two-Year-Old anger is frustration—frustration with her own limits and with the limits that others (especially her parents) impose. She wants to do so much, but so much is denied to her. She becomes angry at her circumstances.

She has preferences and tastes, anxieties and fears, aspirations and temptations, yet everywhere she turns, someone always seems to try to squelch them.

Of course, the ultimate outburst is the temper tantrum. Few Two-Year-Olds make it through the year without a few total breakdowns. Last year, such explosive episodes were often involuntary, a degeneration of control about which the child had little choice. This year, however, tantrums are more likely to be manipulative in nature. For that reason, it's essential to understand this kind of expression of anger so you can cope with it (see Chapter 7).

How to Help

- Permit your child's expression of angry feelings. Control her actions, not her words. If she shows an outburst of anger, reflect back her expressed feelings but don't challenge the feelings themselves: "I can see that you're angry at Joshua. He grabbed your squirt gun and that made you mad."
- When possible, avoid pitched battles with your Two-Year-Old. The more you set up her life for success and self-determination, the less frustration she'll experience.
- When her frustration grows out of some physical challenge, like working a puzzle or reaching an object, offer help. But don't solve all her problems—help just enough to get her back on track.

FEAR

Fear is a familiar emotion in Two-Year-Olds. And in a way, that's a good thing. Very young children are naturally wary about the unfamiliar. An infant cries at sudden loud noises, and flinches if she feels she might fall. Last year, as a One-Year-Old, your child may have expressed fear at big dogs, or the dark, or the faces of unfamiliar adults. For the most part, her fears were fairly concrete.

This year she may still have fears of the concrete variety, including dogs, noisy vacuum cleaners, thunder, unfamiliar bugs. But her growing ability to think, to imagine, to play "what if?", will change the face of her fears. She will be able to create all manner of scary things in her mind, from monsters under the bed to Mommy disappearing to the growly lion that's waiting on page seven of the fairy tale book.

Generally, Two-Year-Olds come to terms with many of their concrete fears as the year progresses. By year's end, they are more likely to focus on imaginary fears.

At the same time, she may experience worries and anxieties that are part and parcel of growing older and wiser.

As her reasoning power and her experience grow, your Two-Year-Old will begin to get a sense of how small and powerless she really is, and how huge and complicated the world is. Not only are there big dogs down the street, there are huge airplanes and noisy trucks and adult conversations that sound kind of scary and huge stores where someone as small as she could get lost.

Unlike you, she can't avoid situations that distress her. If you're afraid of the dentist, you can put it off; she may be afraid of the doctor, but you make her go whether she likes it or not.

At Two, many toddlers' ability to imagine so outstrips their store of knowledge that they become confused about what's possible and what's not. In an effort to make sense of a world that they only partially understand, they engage in what's called "magical" think-ing—attributing human intentions and feelings to inanimate objects, for example, or worrying that they may have caused something bad to happen: death, sep-aration, injury, all manner of worrisome things.

Most concrete fears are fairly easily resolved over time. Your Two-Year-Old may become more comfort-able with dogs after she had gained experience with an assortment of small, friendly pet dogs, or if you have read stories to her about nice dogs. What was once un-familiar and worrisome has become familiar and com-fortable.

But sometimes, fears only intensify. They become en-tirely irrational and begin to interfere with the child's everyday habits. No longer garden-variety fears, they are now phobias.

There is a distinction. Kate, for example, is frightened, but not phobic, of dogs. She's been uncomfortable around them ever since she was knocked over by an overenthusiastic Labrador. She is beginning to conquer her fear as she gets to know other, smaller, less threat-ening dogs. If she and her mother are walking on the street and a large dog approaches, Kate still whimpers and goes into her fear stance—shoulders rigid, elbows bent, fists clenched. Once the dog is out of the picture, however, Kate is cheerful and not particularly fearful.

Marissa, however, worries about dogs constantly. She doesn't want to go out for fear she might meet a dog. She talks about dogs in a fearful voice. She refuses to look at books about animals because there might be a picture of a dog. Marissa's normal fear has intensified to the point that it takes over more and more of her life, and begins to dampen her enthusiasm.

Yet phobias like Marissa's are quite common in Two-Year-Olds. Some psychologsts believe they indicate unresolved anger, and that the thing feared represents the child's discomfort with her own unacceptable anger. Whatever their underlying meaning, phobias among Two-Year-Olds are not necessarily a sign of deep emotional troubles.

Typical Two-Year-Old Fears

- Extremes of size, noise, or pace. Two-Year-Olds often become overwhelmed by anything that seems out of control. An airplane taking off, a trumpeting elephant at the zoo, a jostling crowd, or a violent thunderstorm can make a child feel besieged and off balance.
- Bathtub drains may still upset Two-Year-Olds, who are becoming aware that when things disappear, they go somewhere else. Even toddlers who don't fear the water draining from the tub may well be intensely curious about where it goes.
- Broken or imperfect things. Some Two-Year-Olds will refuse to play with a broken doll, or even refuse to eat a cookie unless it's whole.
- An unusual voice. One Two-Year-Old in day care dissolved into tears every time his beloved teacher used a gruff voice for the Papa Bear when she reads about Goldilocks and the Three Bears to the class.
- Death or separation. Two-Year-Olds do not have a clear understanding of death, because the concept is abstract. But they do understand separation, and may begin to worry about death in terms of a long separation from a loved one.

- Snakes, mice, and insects. For the most part, these are learned fears. Children are rarely frightened of animals (especially small, quiet animals) if the creatures are presented to them as wonders of nature.
- Monsters, witches, bad guys, or other creepy denizens of nightmares. The fear of nightmares itself can sometimes contribute to sleep difficulties.

As normal as fears and phobias are in Two-Year-Olds, they still are upsetting and unpleasant. You will want to do everything you can to prevent fears when possible.

An Ounce of Prevention

- Recognize the distinction between wariness, which is a healthy caution, and a real fear. Respect your Two-Year-Old's caution in a new situation—going down the slide, for example—and she is less likely to become truly fearful.
- Talk to your child about the new experiences in her life, and listen to her questions and concerns. The more she knows, the less she is likely to worry about the unknown.
- Don't dwell on all the dangers that are out there, real as they may be. Emphasize safety, but don't be obsessed.
- Be vigilant about what she views on television or in movies. Adults and older children can put professional wrestling, rock videos, or the evening news broadcast into context. To a Two-Year-Old, images of violence or aggression can be highly distressing.
- Be mindful of your own fears and phobias. You may

not much like spiders yourself, but try to avoid passing your fear along to your child.

How to Help

Your efforts at prevention will probably reduce your child's fears but not entirely eliminate them. Most childhood fears are normal and harmless from a psychological standpoint, but you want to ease them as much as possible.

- Talk with your child about her fears and worries, helping her sort out real from unreal. This will help reduce the distorted information that can generate Two-Year-Old fears.
- Respect your child's fear without legitimizing it. Matt, at twenty-eight months, is frightened by the water going down the bathtub drain. His parents respond by allowing him to get out of the tub before unplugging the drain, so he doesn't have to be frightened. But they also talk to him and say, "I know that scares you, so we'll get you out first. But you know what, Matt? That's just the water going out. Nothing's going to happen to you."
- Don't use fear as a means of discipline. Scary threats (like policemen whisking naughty children off to jail) make children fearful, but do little to improve their behavior.
- Don't force a fearful child into a feared situation. If your child is reluctant to go into the swimming pool, don't make her. If she is allowed plenty of time to

move at her own pace, her own desire for fun may eventually overcome her fearfulness.

- If your Two-Year-Old is afraid of the dark, use a nightlight to calm her fears. Or leave a lamp on at night, reducing the wattage of the bulb over time until she will accept an ordinary nightlight.

- Don't force bravery. Little boys, especially, can feel intense pressure to be brave, "a big boy," in a situation that frightens them. Ironically, this kind of pressure may ultimately make a child more fearful and tense, because in addition to his original fear, he has to worry about disappointing you and not measuring up.

- Anxieties that relate to a child's sense of vulnerability can be eased by reading stories about the real world. Select books that show that the big world out there is interesting, attractive, and orderly.

- Fantasy play helps, too. You might help her initiate a play scenario in which she is big, brave and powerful. This lets her practice the feelings of fearlessness in a safe setting.

- If your child screams in fear at night, but doesn't seem to respond to you or be aware of her surroundings, she may be experiencing a night terror. Night terrors are less common than nightmares, and differ from them in other ways: the child doesn't usually waken fully, even though her eyes are open; she is difficult to comfort; and she has no memory of the scary episode the next day. The best treatment is to stay with her and comfort her until she falls back to sleep.

- When your Two-Year-Old wakes up with a nightmare, concentrate on alleviating her fear, not setting her straight about what's real and what's not. If she dreams about monsters, the dream monsters are just as scary to her as real monsters would be to you. If she is still anxious even after you've soothed her, offer to chase away the monsters. Next morning is a good time to talk about the difference between reality and fantasy.

PRIDE AND SELF-ESTEEM

Don't worry about overconfidence at this age. The more wonderful your child thinks she is, the better. That's not to say she should never be thwarted, follow rules, or consider other people's feelings. But she doesn't have to be taught humility right now. She feels small and humble enough on her own.

Your child may approach a new acquaintance with the announcement that she can put her own shoes on (when she can't). Or she may, especially later in the year, elaborate and exaggerate her accomplishments. "I can build it all the way up to here," she says disdainfully, watching another child struggle with a construction of blocks.

How to Help

- Don't discourage your child if she boasts and swaggers a bit. As with her fears, you don't have to buy into her delusions of grandeur or accept them as real. Instead, acknowledge her feelings. If she says she's going to climb to the top of the pine tree, you can say, "You ARE getting to be pretty good at climbing, aren't you!"

- Talk about when she was a baby and how far she's come since then.
- Tell stories with her as the heroine, and see if she'll tell a story about herself.
- Praise her for her efforts, rather than focusing exclusively on her accomplishments. When she builds a sand castle, you can point out, "I see you figured out a way to keep that part from falling. Good work!"
- Be generous with praise, but don't go overboard. Praise doesn't have to be effusive in order to be effective.
- Be mindful how you talk about your child in her hearing. She believes in you so strongly that she will take quite seriously the way you describe her to others.

GENDER AND SEXUALITY

By Two, most children understand that they are either a boy or a girl. During bath time, and as diapers come off in preparation for toilet learning, children become aware of, and interested in, their own genitals and those of others. Your Two-Year-Old probably will be most interested in the structural differences of men's and women's bodies, but may not be much interested in lectures about adult sexual function. You can help your Two-Year-Old develop a positive attitude toward her body by making sure she knows the names for all body parts—her own and those that belong to the opposite sex. You can say, "Those are your nipples. That's your vagina. That's David's penis."

Two-Year-Olds may masturbate for pleasure or curiosity and be curious about other bodies, both child and adult. You can let your child know that touching private parts is okay when she's by herself, but that it's not grown-up to do so in front of others. If she does, distraction (by putting a toy in her hand, for example) may be more effective than stern warnings.

Learning these rules is no more likely to repress your child's sexuality than learning simple table manners will repress her enjoyment of food. And at Two, the rules can be quite simple indeed: "Babies don't have to wear clothes in the ocean," you can say, "but big girls wear a bathing suit, just like Mommy."

JEALOUSY AND SIBLING RIVALRY

Most Two-Year-Old jealousy is aimed at a new baby. The arrival of a new sibling throws your child off balance in several ways. First, her beloved routine will probably be quite disrupted for awhile. Second, her close bond with you may seem threatened. It's not surprising that most Twos do not always view the new arrival with grace and generosity.

If you do have a second child this year, do all you can to help your Two-Year-Old weather the stress of suddenly having to share you.

How to Help

• Prepare your Two-Year-Old for the impending event by talking to her about the baby, where the baby is growing, and what it will be like to have a new baby in the house.

- Don't overdo the preparations. Two-Year-Olds are just beginning to understand future events. If you get too specific early in your pregnancy, though, by the ninth month she may think this is never going to happen.
- Prepare your child for the period of separation by getting her accustomed to the person who will care for her while you're away.
- Let your Two-Year-Old see some new babies, so she won't have unrealistic expectations when the baby arrives. If you have told her she's going to have ''a new brother or sister to play with,'' she will be quite disappointed with what you bring home from the hospital.
- If your Two-Year-Old will have to move to a different bedroom, or from a crib to a bed, try to make the move several months before the baby arrives. If the move occurs immediately before the baby's arrival, it will seem more like a displacement.
- Allow your Two-Year-Old to visit you in the hospital.
- When you arrive home, let someone else hold the new baby for a moment while you reconnect with your Two-Year-Old.
- Appeal to her sense of pride by allowing her to participate in the baby's care.
- Encourage her to talk about her feelings. If she is annoyed by the baby, she can tell you that. Be sympathetic, and acknowledge that new babies are sometimes disruptive and bothersome.
- No matter how much she seems to love the baby, she can't yet be trusted alone with him. Two-Year-Olds do act roughly with little babies, and your supervision will keep the baby safe and protect your older child from acting on her jealous impulses.

SHAME

Many Two-Year-Olds show a well-developed sense of shame, especially when they are caught violating some rule and incurring your disapproval. Some sensitive children are so aware of this sensation that they wilt at the slightest tone of disapproval in your voice.

Others, however, seem impervious to shame. Patrick, for example, is caught in the act of scribbling on the wall. His outraged mother scolds him heartily, but Patrick does not seem the least bit ashamed of himself. His major concern is the possibility of punishment, not any sense of having done wrong.

An awareness of having violated the rules and expectations of loved ones is the foundation on which your child will, eventually, construct a sense of right and wrong. She will, ultimately, learn to internalize these rules and expectations. When that happens—several years later—she will have what we call a conscience.

But at Two, your child is a beginner. The kind of remorse and guilt that can goad adults to evaluate and improve their behavior is beyond her. Whether she wilts under your disapproval or has a hide of leather, she will learn more from your gentle reminders about rules than she will from any effort to shame or humiliate her.

However, you can talk about the feeling of shame with your Two-Year-Old, just as you talk about other feelings and emotions. You can talk about how people feel when they've done something that isn't right. You can model those feelings yourself by talking about your

117

own errors or mistakes, how they make you feel, and what actions you take to make things right.

But a sense of conscience—an internalization of a sense of right and wrong—won't develop for quite a few more years. So your Two-Year-Old is unlikely to be plagued by a sense of guilt.

EMOTIONS AND PLAY

As your Two-Year-Old's ability to play socially and imaginatively increase this year, she will increasingly incorporate emotions into her play. She and her fellow Twos may reenact a domestic scene in which orders are issued and refused, someone gets punished, and someone gets put to bed with a hug and a kiss. She can play out her fears and try fanciful responses to them in a risk-free setting. It's advisable to encourage this process by nurturing her developing creative and imaginative abilities (see "Imagination," Chapter 3), and helping her acquire the vocabulary she will need for emotional exchanges.

TIME CAPSULES
24 Months

For most children, the emotional waters are fairly calm at this age. Two-Year-Olds are often cuddly, affectionate, and fairly cooperative. Fears at this stage are mostly of the concrete kind: thunder, vacuum cleaners, and other noisy things, plus big dogs. Strange and unfamiliar situations may also inspire fear. Resistance to your wishes is still mostly physical (running or pulling away), rather than verbal.

30 Months

At midyear, your Two-Year-Old may well be on an emotional roller coaster. She's made up of extremes, mood swings, wild changes between clinging and resisting. She's indecisive and has trouble making choices. She is much more resistant, demanding, and rigid. She shows more tension and anxiety, and tantrums increase.

36 Months

By year's end, your Two-Year-Old's emotions will still be strong, but her ability to cope with them will increase. She is becoming somewhat less rigid, less resistant, more able to control her own behavior and comply with your expectations. She still resists, but is more likely to state her resistance verbally and even attempt to negotiate. Her imaginative play sequences are more realistic and planned. As her imagination develops, her fears become more imaginative: witches, monsters, fierce animals. Nightmares become more frequent.

QUESTIONS AND ANSWERS

Q: *My Two-Year-Old is not particularly fearful, but he gets upset at strange-sounding voices. If I use a very different voice when I'm playing with him or reading* *him a story, he acts scared and tells me to stop. Why does this bother him?*

A: He's probably reacting to your strange voice the same way many Two-Year-Olds reacted when they see their parent put on a Halloween mask: He doesn't like anything about you to be suddenly unfamiliar. One of the most comforting thing about you this year is your predictability and sameness, and he dislikes the idea of you not being YOU. When he's older, changes in your voice and appearance probably won't bother him.

Q: *My daughter becomes hysterical during thunderstorms. She isn't concerned about the lightning, but she starts screaming as soon as the thunder begins. I've tried to explain to her that it won't hurt her, that it's just a loud noise. Nothing seems to calm her down. What can we do?*

A: Fear of thunder is very common among Two-Year-Olds. For some, the sudden booms are so uncomfortable that they seem like pain. If you then talk about how the thunder won't hurt her, you don't seem sympathetic to her plight. Try to eliminate the noise as much as possible by closing windows, then stay with her during the storm. Later, talk about weather with her. At that time, you can help her understand that the thunder and lightning won't do her any harm.

Q: *My twenty-eight-month-old-son doesn't engage in any pretend play. He plays with his trucks, but he mostly just chugs them around. He doesn't create any stories the way his sister did at that age. Is there anything I can do to help him?*

A: Most children of your son's age are moving toward greater involvement in pretend and emotional play, but some don't begin until later in the year. If he is doing well in other areas, he may just need practice. You can help him progress, however, by going back to the previous milestones described in this chapter. If he has not introduced emotional ideas into his play, perhaps he needs more practice with simple imitative play. If he is able to use a toy saw to "saw" a board, or a play kitchen to prepare food, you can become a partner in his play and guide his imitative play into imitative sequences, and, from there, gradually into stories (see, also, suggestions for enhancing imagination in Chapter 3).

7

The Taming of the Two: Setting Limits

As a parent, you have the right to set limits, to say no, to establish some patterns and rules in your home that not only keep your child safe but also help you retain your sanity. Of course that's not always easy, and you'll continue to compromise and sacrifice this year as you did since he was born.

People are different, and they come to parenting with different histories and philosophies. You'll need to choose an approach to setting limits that fits your personality and your child's. If you're naturally patient and tolerant, and your child responds well to reason, your approach can be fairly relaxed. If you have a short fuse and your child delights in igniting it, you may have to establish more strict rules and expectations. If you aren't comfortable with the pattern of discipline that you are trying to use, it won't be effective. Your heart won't be in it, and you won't use it consistently.

But whatever approach you use, you do have a right and obligation to teach your Two-Year-Old ways of behaving and getting on in the world. You want him to end this year with some understanding of limits, with an ability to control his behavior some of the time, and an interest in cooperating with adult expectations some of the time.

Because by his Third birthday, he will have established patterns of behavior that will shape his attitude toward authority in general and parental guidelines in particular. With luck, he will have a reasonable respect for authority, but not a blind, fearful obedience.

But first, you have to get from here to there. And "here" can be a challenge indeed.

Seth, who is twenty-eight months old, usually picks the moment when his mother is trying to prepare dinner to creep into the kitchen, climb up on a chair, and reach for the sharp knives he knows he's not supposed to touch. When his mother catches him and shoos him out the door, he sneaks back in, opens the refrigerator, and empties as much of the contents as he can before she drops what she's doing and stops him.

But this is no longer the innocent, exuberant exploring that Seth did as a One-Year-Old. Seth is disobeying on purpose, and it's driving his mother crazy.

"He needs constant supervision," she says with a sigh. "Making dinner turns into trying to watch him, trying to cook, and cleaning up whatever he spilled. Whenever he gets his hands on something he shouldn't, he gets that look in his eye to see when you're going to explode."

The Terrible Twos are the stuff of legend, cartoons, jokes, and tall tales. Perfect strangers will chuckle knowingly when you tell them your child has just turned Two.

Next to coping with adolescence, everyone says, surviving a Two-Year-Old is supposed to be the toughest job parents face.

These can be frightening words, especially if your cherubic One-Year-Old has just turned Two and seems to be just as cheerful, jolly, and full of sunshine as ever. Could your little angel really sprout horns right before your eyes?

Take heart! The Terribleness of the Twos is overrated (and so, for that matter, are the Terrible Teens). Despite some inevitable hard times, many parents look back on Two as one of the best years. Their children came alive in so many ways. Twos could understand, talk, and think. They were truly children, no longer babies.

Still, there are good reasons for this to be a ticklish year when it comes to your child's behavior. He has a specific agenda of things he needs to accomplish this year. That agenda brings with it some special challenges. And yet you'll be able to use some new techniques for guiding that you didn't have last year.

THE TWO'S AGENDA

Your Two-Year-Old has substantial developmental tasks to accomplish this year. Among them are the following:

- He needs to assert his individuality—to announce to the world (and to himself) that he is a real person, someone to be reckoned with. This drives him to throw his weight around from time to time.
- He has to gain your approval by doing what you want

125

and not doing what you don't want. He needs to feel capable of pleasing you, at least some of the time. This need will encourage him to accept the limits you set.

- He needs to learn to control his behavior and resist temptation, at least some of the time.
- He needs to learn acceptable ways of influencing other people, especially powerful people like you.
- For better or worse, this year he will form his own attitudes and approach toward authority. By the end of this year he will have established whether, in later life, he is likely to be fearful and overly compliant, resistant and hostile, or capable of that delicate balance of assertiveness and cooperation that will serve him best.

THE CHALLENGE

You don't want your Two-Year-Old to stay the way he is forever. You want him to grow and change. But becoming civilized can be a messy process. If you have to break a few eggs to make an omelet, your Two-Year-Old will have to break some old patterns of attachment and behavior in order to move forward.

First, he can't learn all those rules and expectations unless he knows what will happen if he disobeys them; he can't respect limits until he has established exactly where they are. That means he will test your rules and limits, along with your patience.

This testing process is a kind of experimentation, an extension of the experiments he conducted with such physical objects as blocks and sand last year. When Seth opens the drawer and takes out a forbidden kitchen knife, he is testing how serious his parents' rules are, how vigilant they are, and what their response will be.

Similarly, your Two-Year-Old will experiment with ways to infuence you and make you do what he wants. He will try both positive and negative approaches. He will try to get a cookie by saying please, and he will also try by grabbing, screaming, or whining.

THE LANGUAGE OF LIMITS

Brendan's parents knew their son had left infancy behind him when they realized they were starting to spell "ice cream" in his presence. "From the time they're born, you get used to living with a little guy who doesn't really understand what you're talking about," said Brendan's father. "Now we have to consider what we say and how we say it.

And in matters of setting limits, the words you choose make a difference in how your Two-Year-Old perceives himself. For example, it's best not to discuss his behavior with other people when he's around, unless your comments are positive. And it's wise, when speaking to your child, to select words that focus on his behavior, rather than inherent virtue. A Two-Year-Old who misbehaves is not bad; he has forgotten a rule or made the wrong choice.

And the words you use to describe punishment should be selected with care, too. Some parents prefer the term "consequence": "Brendan, Dad told you to stay off the soccer field during your brother's game. If you run out again, there will be a consequence."

YOUR EXPANDING REPERTOIRE

Fortunately, you have many strengths to draw on as you face these challenges. For one thing, you have experience. You have successfully raised your child for his first two years, which is indeed no small accomplishment.

Many of the techniques you found successful last year will still serve you well. But because your Two-Year-Old has new skills and abilities, you have some new ways to help him behave.

- His longer memory means that he can remember rules better.
- His emerging understanding of cause and effect means that he can think about what might happen if he misbehaves.
- His increased language ability means he can understand what you tell him.
- His developing autonomy includes a sense of pride and a desire to please you; he is eager to become a member of the civilized world and to enjoy all the rights and privileges thereof.
- His rigidity and obsession with ritual can be an advantage as you teach him limits and socially acceptable ways. He is ready to develop habits of civilized behavior that will serve him in years to come.

Of course, with all these new strengths, you also have some more difficult tasks:

- You can no longer outsmart your child in conflict situations: distractions won't work nearly as well. If you try that old "Look! Over there! A bunny!" technique that may have worked when your child was One, you're likely to get a pained expression that says "Yeah, right."
- More scheming and manipulative behavior develops this year. Your child is aware of pretense, of his ability to influence others. At first, he won't be very skilled at it.

MOTHER (smelling suspicious diaper odor): Patrick, do you need a diaper change?
PATRICK: NO!

Later, he may try negotiation and arguing.

MOTHER: Time for bath, Patrick. Let's go.
PATRICK: I'm a horsey. Horsey doesn't take a bath."

Overall, your approach toward setting reasonable limits for your Two-Year-Old needs to evolve with his growing abilities. He responds well to order and routine, but he can dig in his heels and resist you with new vigor. He can demand the right to express his opinions and his preferences, but then freeze when he's asked to make a choice.

As with last year, you should take advantage of household engineering that makes life easier for everyone. You will want to prioritize your rules, focusing on the most important ones—relating to safety, or your own sanity—and easing up on the less important matters, such as tidiness and table manners.

Remember, also, that consequences for negative behavior do not need to be harsh in order to be effective.

They certainly should be unpleasant, something your child would rather avoid. But harsh punishment is actually less effective than fair, consistent, moderate discipline.

And, finally, you need to develop a sixth sense for when to lighten up, to be flexible, to let him win an occasional battle. Going head to head with your Two-Year-Old to "show him who's boss" usually just ends up with everyone getting upset (and you may be surprised to find out who's boss!).

TECHNIQUES THAT WORK (SOME OF THE TIME)
Engineering Better Behavior

Presumably, you have been through the intricacies of baby-proofing and child proofing your home (see Chapter 10 for more on this subject). But the way you organize your home can also contribute to your Two-Year-Old's ability to behave.

Last year or before, you probably moved most breakables out of his reach and restricted his access to rooms or areas where he could cause trouble. Your aim then was provide him with a "safe zone" where he could roam and touch and play without too much restriction.

To a great extent, you can continue that approach this year. You need to keep your child safe, you need to protect your own possessions, and he needs the freedom to explore without hearing a constant chorus of "Be careful!" and "Don't touch!" And don't lead him into temptation, with all sorts of intriguing knickknacks in his reach that you don't want him to handle.

But this year, he does need to learn some rules and

begin to resist some temptations. He is actually interested in the idea of property, and who owns what, and what belongs where. This year, you might want to introduce a few items that may tempt him but he isn't supposed to touch (maybe the television remote control), or that he can ask you for permission to touch (a figurine). Be sure to explain what you expect of him, and praise him for his successes. If he fails consistently, you can say you have to put the item away until he's older. If he succeeds, you can gradually trust him with more.

Explain Yourself

Now that your Two-Year-Old is a fairly verbal creature, it makes sense to explain the rules in words. Always tell him a rule before you begin enforcing it. You might say, "Now that you're almost Three, you don't need to grab the bread off the plate. You're old enough to ask for it, like big boys do." Be sure, also, to remind your Two-Year-Old of policies and rules ahead of time when you're about to take him somewhere special, like a restaurant or a store. If you tell him on the way into the restaurant that "we don't sing in restaurants," he'll remember that fairly easily. He'll have a much harder time if you wait until he bursts into song and *then* explain the rule.

Present a United Front

Not only both parents, but other caregivers should enforce the same limits. Your Two-Year-Old is learning rapidly how to get what he wants from people, and he will take advantage of any weakness he spots in the alliance. If one of you allows him to scamper freely up and down the supermarket aisles and the other doesn't, he'll have trouble taking either of you seriously.

On the other hand, parents are people, and people are different. It's not a bad thing for your child to learn, for example, that Dad is grouchy in the morning, or that Mommy is always a pushover to read just one more story. Becoming sensitive to the individuality of other people will serve him well in life.

Behave Yourself

When possible, do model appropriate behavior yourself. If you have set firm rules about candy and in-between-meal snacks for your child, try to abide by them yourself. Of course, there are times when you have to say "Do as I say, not as I do". After all, you are allowed to use the power mower and the sewing machine, and he's not. But your Two-Year-Old is able to notice how you behave, and whether you respect safety and other rules.

Redirect with Words

Last year, you redirected your One-Year-Old away from trouble by taking advantage of his distractability. This year, he's not quite so easily distracted. It may still work on occasion, but you'll have better luck by distracting him with words, not actions. If he's busy resisting having his boots put on, try talking, as you continue to put the boots on, about something interesting, such as all the fun you'll have together once he gets into his snowsuit and boots.

You can still divert him with a "change of scene." This is particularly helpful if you sense trouble brewing in the sandbox; everyone is getting rowdy, the noise and fatigue levels are cranking up, and you fear that tantrums will break out any moment. This is the time to propose a snack break.

Take Advantage of His Love of Routine

Your Two-Year-Old is learning that there is a right way to do things at the same time that he loves doing things the same way. Try, if you can, to get him to view rules and limits as habits and routines. He can climb into his car seat and help you with the seat belt. He can be the official reminder who asks if everybody is buckled up before the car starts. He can make a habit of reaching for your hand as you prepare to cross the street, or saying "Excuse me" instead of interrupting. He won't fight you about activities that he is used to and comfortable with.

Give Second Chances

If you give an order and your Two-Year-Old refuses, offer him a second chance. You can say, "I've asked you to stop pulling the leaves off that plant, Ryan. Do you need a second chance?" This gives him a face-

133

saving way to stop the unsuitable behavior. However, two chances are enough. If he still disobeys after two, his behavior needs a more serious treatment.

The Time-Honored Time-Out

The Time-Out is an effective way of dealing with a child who is disobeying deliberately. If you have explained the rules, tried distraction, and issued a second chance, now is the time for a Time-Out. Here is how it works:

- Announce Time-Out, and tell your child the reason for it.
- Remove him from the scene of the crime and place him in his room or a neutral place away from the action.
- Put a portable kitchen timer near the Time-Out place and set it for two or three minutes (roughly one minute per year of age, so you can increase the length a bit over the year).
- Leave him alone. Do not talk to him or beg him to behave.
- If he leaves the Time-Out place or begins to kick and scream, go back, reset the timer, and start over.
- When the Time-Out is over, welcome him back calmly. Let bygones be bygones.
- If he repeats the behavior, repeat the Time-Out.

TECHNIQUES THAT DON'T USUALLY WORK
Screaming

What? You say you have actually raised your voice to your child? Of course you have, and you probably will again. Even the best of parents do, on occasion. But yelling at a child will not improve his behavior. And if yelling becomes a habit, it is not only unpleasant for parent and child alike, it also crowds out much more effective ways of managing your Two-Year-Old's behavior.

If you scream and yell and then don't follow through with any action, your Two-Year-Old will quickly learn that your ranting is a show that he needs to sit through before he gets his way. It becomes another Two-Year-Old routine: "I pull the cat's tail. Then Mommy yells for awhile. Then I pull the cat's tail again." It's not easy when you're angry, but it's better to tell him what he did wrong and issue an appropriate consequence. It's okay, also, to let him know that you feel angry.

Spanking

As with screaming, it is probably a rare parent who gets through the toddler years without ever, ever, swatting a diapered bottom. But while a rare, decisive spank when a child has violated a serious rule (like struggling out of his car seat while you're driving) may have some merit, frequent spanking does not improve behavior. Here's why:

- It undermines the sense of cooperation that you are trying to instill in your child this year. You want your child to feel that both of you are on the same side. Harsh punishment and spanking cast you as adversaries.
- It tends to escalate. If spanking becomes your primary means of controlling your Two-Year-Old, what do you do next?
- Harsh punishment of any kind seems to be associated, over time, with higher aggression in children (see "The Too-Aggressive Child," below).

ALL TALK, NO ACTION

Parents of Two-Year-Olds are at risk of providing too much explanation to their children. This is understandable, because for the first time, your child really can understand quite a bit of what you tell him. And you do need to to explain rules and expectations to him. Many is the parent who has separated a pair of squabbling Two-Year-Olds with a lecture: "Now Michael, if you take Andrew's truck while he's still trying to use it, you will make Andrew sad and he won't like you and he won't invite you over to his house, and you won't get to play in his new wading pool and then you'll be all sad and. . . . '' Stop! Get a grip!

Yes, words are more and more important this year. But Two-Year-Olds quickly tune out to long explanations that string together a series of ever-more-distant consequences. Better to say, "Michael, Andrew is still using the truck. You can use this race car until Andrew is finished. Then it will be your turn."

Begging on Bended Knee

"Aaron, go back to bed. Please go to bed. You're tired, and so is Mommy. Won't you please get back in your bed?" When Aaron's mother begs him to go back to bed by saying "please," her intention is partly to get him to obey, and partly to reinforce good manners by modeling polite words. But she is actually reinforcing a confusing idea for a Two-Year-Old. She is changing the balance of power. As his parent, she has the right to set up the bedtime expectations. By wheedling, she appears to be opening the rules up to negotiation.

Her message sounds more confident if she says, "Aaron, it's time for you to be in bed. Let's get you back under the covers."

Setting Expectations Too High

Tyler's mother had just set out a dessert buffet in the dining room. Then she went upstairs to get tidied up before the guests arrived. When she returned, Tyler had partaken freely of petit fours, eclairs, and little iced cookies.

"I told him to leave the food alone," she told the guests apologetically. "He never listens."

Actually, Tyler did listen. For a brief moment, he really intended to do as his mother asked. But the siren call of all those treats simply drowned out her words. Two-Year-Olds are not good at resisting temptation. They haven't mastered the interior dialogue most of us use to build up our resistance: "I know that looks good, but I'd better not. Mommy will get mad if I take one now. If I obey her, she might let me have some later."

You'll have an easier time with your Two-Year-Old if you recognize his limitations and set your expectations at an age-appropriate level. If you take him into an antique shop and say, "Don't touch," he may not be able to resist all the fascinating, breakable, expensive items on display. It makes more sense to spare him, yourself, and the shop owner, needless stress.

Yes and No Questions

"Jamie! Do you want to take a bath?"

"Are you going to eat your broccoli, dear?"

"Do you want to put your blocks away now so we can get ready for bed?"

Three guesses what the answer would be to those questions. Two-Year-Olds, especially at midyear, are eager to find ways to assert themselves. If you pose a yes/no question, you are sure to get the answer you don't want. And then you've got yourself into a conflict that might have been avoided. A more effective way to get your child to go along with the program is to use "Let's" phrases, as in, "Let's get these blocks off the floor so Daddy won't trip over them."

Shaming

As we said in Chapter 6, your child pays close attention to what you say about him. So if he's been a holy terror all day, try to wait until he's out of the room before you expound on his sins to your spouse at the end of the day.

It's better, also, not to tell him he ought to be ashamed of himself because he flushed his sister's Little Pony down the toilet. You certainly can proceed with whatever consequence you would use for this infraction, but you'll both do better if you keep shame out of it. He doesn't really know how to feel ashamed yet. After all, he probably enjoyed doing it, and the only reason he's sorry is because he got caught.

Johnny Be Good

Asking your Two-Year-Old to be "good" is not likely to be helpful at this age. If you say, "Now be a good boy in the store," he may nod and agree, but he doesn't yet have a clear idea of all that being "good" entails. Your encouraging pep talk should be as specific as possible: "We're going to hold hands in here. Remember, this is a 'No-touch' store. Remember to hold my hand."

Focusing on specific behavior helps him get a clear idea of what you expect, and it also puts the emphasis on the behavior, where it belongs, rather than on essential "goodness" or "badness."

COPING WITH "TERRIBLE TWO" TANTRUMS

Chances are that by the time you find yourself the proud parent of a Two-Year-Old, you've fought your way through quite a few tantrums. Such meltdowns of self-control are common in One-Year-Olds, and they're often almost involuntary. Two-Year-Olds, however, are more purposeful in all their behavior, and tantrums are no exception.

"Every time we go to to Kmart, he has a major hissy fit when I try to wheel the cart past the toy section," says Patrick's mother. "It's 'Gimme, gimme, gimme!' And when I don't gimme, he blows up. When that happens, I just grab him and bail out. I once left a whole cart full of begonias in the aisle."

Two-Year-Olds are becoming more and more aware of the impact of their behavior on others. Their tantrums grow more deliberate and more goal-oriented. They usually occur when the Two-Year-Old has been thwarted or pressured, and is determined to resist. If you can avoid giving in to tantrums this year, you should see a decrease in frequency.

However, there are other contributing factors. Frustration, stress, and fatigue make tantrums more likely. You may find your child loses control more frequently around the time he gives up one or both of his naps. If you can adjust his schedule and anticipate his buildup of frustration, you may be able to prevent some outbursts.

How to Help

- Try to stay calm during a tantrum. If you dissolve into exasperation or rage, it will feed your Two-Year-Old's fury, rather than defuse it.
- Do not reward tantrums. Resist the temptation to give in just to avoid embarrassment in a public place. Far

better to leave a cart full of begonias at Kmart than reinforce a tantrum by buying a toy.

- Don't try to reason with him. During the outburst, your Two-Year-Old is not likely to listen to reason.
- If you are capable of ignoring a tantrum while it continues in your presence, do so. If you can't, separate yourself from the fireworks. Sitting there trying to look calm while your child bounces off the walls is stressful for you. And you run the risk of becoming an interesting audience, with your fists clenched, your teeth grinding, and smoke coming out of your ears.
- Put your Two-Year-Old in Time-Out and tell him he can come out when he's ready to be calm.
- Do let bygones be bygones. After the tantrum has blown over, let your child start with a clean slate.
- When he's calm, let your child know that this behavior is not acceptable and that you know he will learn to control it eventually.

THE TOO-AGGRESSIVE CHILD

Christopher is becoming an outcast at play group. He grabs, he kicks, punches, pulls, and throws. If the other children are coloring or playing with blocks, he goes on the attack. If his mother or another parent attempts a Time-Out, Christopher aims careful, swift kicks at their knees as they carry him away.

You probably have met a Christopher. If you're lucky, he goes home from play group with some other parent, not you. But even if your child is the highly aggressive one, all is not lost. Aggressive behavior is normal in Two-Year-Olds, and children gain control over their impulses at very different rates this year. Most Christophers really do improve with age.

However, there are extreme situations that call for a concentrated effort:

- If your Two-Year-Old is behaving so violently that other parents won't allow their children to play with him, you'll want to intervene. The long-term risk here is not just the aggression itself, but the lost opportunity for social interaction that this represents, and the toll it will take on your child's self-image.
- If your Two-Year-Old seems to be regressing, or making no progress managing his impulses, you may need to look for other factors in his life that are upsetting him—a recent move, family disruptions, a new sibling. Ideally, even rambunctious Two-Year-Olds should be making some progress this year. (*Note*: Don't consider it regression if your relatively compliant twenty-four-month-old suddenly turns aggressive at thirty months. This is a common pattern, and usually improves by age Three.)
- If your child's aggressiveness is associated with extreme destructiveness or cruelty to animals, you should share your concerns with your pediatrician or a specialist in child behavior.

How to Help

- Work with your child on his social skills. Behaving in a socially acceptable manner is a matter of practice. Chapter 5 describes social skills that you can reasonably expect in a Two-Year-Old.

- Set firm limits on aggression. If your child bites or hits, remove him from the group and explain again that he is not permitted to hurt others. Just because it's understandable for Two-Year-Olds to lose control and behave aggressively does not mean it should be permitted or indulged.
- Explain these limits to your child. Say, "Hitting hurts. We don't allow you to hurt people." That way he understands that even if he loses control, an adult will enforce the peace.
- Let your child know that there are acceptable ways to let all those angry feelings out: Punching a pillow, stomping, saying "I'm mad at you!"
- Cut down on his exposure to violence, either through entertainment or in imitation of older children or adults. Don't glorify fighting. However, do permit healthy expressions of aggression and energy. Make sure he has adequate outlets for his energy.
- Try not to break his spirit as you work on his aggression. Make it clear that it's the hitting, not your child, that you disapprove of.
- Take a close look at your approach to discipline. Are you too lax? Too harsh? Some researchers suggest that extremely aggressive behavior is increased when parents let violent behavior occur, then punish it harshly. Conversely, aggressive behavior is lowest when parents set firm limits about violent or aggressive behavior, but punish gently.

Christopher, for example, is enthralled with violent entertainment and gets large doses of it at home. He is the youngest of three brothers, and the older boys play violent video games and generally glorify roughness and toughness. There's very little message to the contrary in Christopher's homelife. But when his own aggressive behavior gets to the point that his parents have had enough, they administer a vigorous spanking.

TOO GOOD TO BE TRUE?

Imagine a thirty-month-old who never had tantrums, obeyed every command, never once made any trouble for anyone. Sound good? It may be, or it may be a sign of trouble.

Consistently aggressive, disobedient behavior is certainly a problem for Two-Year-Olds and those who must spend time with them. But the absence of all aggression or disobedience is not desirable either. A certain amount of resistance and refusal and testing is to be expected, and the child who never does any of these is telling us that something isn't quite right.

Certainly, Two-Year-Olds vary greatly in how much resistance they display. And some children have a naturally sunny, cooperative disposition that rarely impels them into mischief.

But a child who never disobeys this year may be worried and fearful about losing his parents' approval. A child who seems excessively upset when he makes a mistake or spills or breaks something may need reassurance that he's loved and accepted even when he's not perfect.

QUESTIONS AND ANSWERS

Q: *My neighbor's daughter is very sensitive to criticism from her parents. If her father so much as frowns* *at her, she stops whatever she's doing. My own son doesn't seem to care what we say or think. The only way to deal with him is punishment—and sometimes nothing works. Doesn't he care that we're unhappy with him?*

A: As we discussed in Chapter 6, some children are more sensitive to disapproval than others. Your neighbor's daughter may just be naturally sensitive, or she may be excessively worried about her ability to please her parents and retain their love.

Your son may require a firmer hand than your neighbor's daughter, but that doesn't mean he doesn't value your good opinion. Even the most Terrible of Twos still need lots of love, affection, and approval. Over time, as he learns more control and you continue to praise him for his good behavior, he will be more responsive to your displeasure.

Q: *My two-and-a-half-year-old daughter keeps going into our bathroom and getting into my perfume and makeup, no matter how many times I tell her not to. My husband thinks she just isn't old enough to know better, but I think she is because of the way she looks at me when I catch her. Is she doing this on purpose?*

A: Your daughter is probably old enough to understand quite well that she is expected to leave your things alone. If she really didn't understand initially, she certainly did after you scolded her the first time.

Your course of action depends on several considerations. How serious an offense is this? Is she doing it to get your attention—or your goat? Or is she doing it because she is genuinely interested in all the neat stuff you have in there?

Among your options, depending on your conclusions, are:

- Putting temptation out of her reach.
- Providing her with a child's cosmetic kit of her own.
- Giving her a Time-Out when she violates the rule.

Q: *My niece, who is almost Three, has started telling us things that we know aren't true. Recently, she insisted that she knows how to read, which she doesn't. Then she showed me her big brother's tricycle and said he'd given it to her and it was hers now. Her parents just laugh it off. Shouldn't they be teaching her to tell the truth?*

A: At Two and Three, children are just beginning to sense the difference between fiction and nonfiction. They're beginning to understand that it's possible to fool people by saying something that isn't true. Sometimes, when they pretend, adults are delighted. Other times, adults get upset. It's very hard to sort all this out at Three, and your niece's behavior is quite normal. Over time, she'll learn the virtues of truthfulness, and when pretend is all in fun and when it's dishonest. Right now, there's no need to correct your niece or discourage her. Instead, you can validate her interest in books and tricycles by saying, "Boy, you do like books, don't you! So do I!" or, "I can see you want a BIG tricycle!"

8

Rites of Passage:
The Daily Rhythms of Your
Two-Year-Old's Life

Between her second and third birthday, your child will take over responsibility for more and more of her own daily care. She will feed herself with greater skill, put on some of her own clothes, wash and dry her hands, and at least begin the process of giving up diapers.

As she struggles with all the new skills she must learn and with all the burdens of growing into a more independent creature, she will take a few steps forward and a few steps back as she veers between striving for independence and clinging to her familiar sources of comfort.

One moment she will insist on putting on her shoes all by herself, even when she can't manage the task. The next, she will refuse to feed herself, even though she's been using a fork and spoon for several months.

As always, her greatest source of comfort and reassurance will be you. But this year, she will typically develop a new way of feeling secure in her rapidly changing world. She will yearn for sameness and predictability. She will, in fact, try to impose order on her life by putting things in the same place, by doing things in the same order, even by following the same route through the house. She will become upset if any aspect of this comforting order is disrupted.

This typical Two-Year-Old love of sameness takes many forms:

- Anthony sleeps with his shoes on.
- Maria loves bubbles in her bath, but won't get into the tub unless all the bubbles are pushed to the far end.
- Molly can't sleep unless a blue leather-bound volume of de Tocqueville is placed just so on her bureau.
- Carlos takes the lids off his plastic toy bins and carefully leans them against the wall in exactly the same spot every time.
- Adam's good-night ritual calls for his mother reciting, in chronological order, the birthday of every member of his family.

In this chapter, we'll examine the developmental forces that underlie your Two-Year-Old's passion for order this year. We'll look at how you can work with this tendency as you guide your child toward greater independence. And then we'll look at that process during some of the major routines of your child's day.

HOW ROUTINES SERVE YOUR TWO-YEAR-OLD'S NEEDS

Carlos, at two-and-a-half, likes to have a place for everything and everything in its place. Inside one of those plastic bins, he has vehicles—and only vehicles. In another, he keeps plastic people and animals. Certain categories of toys stay up in his room, and are to be played with only in his room. Others are for living room play. If some thoughtless adult should move a living room toy to the bedroom, Carlos indignantly fetches it and returns it to its proper place.

Sometimes, a child's firm sense of where things belong can be misinterpreted as a social failing. Alex is in the community swimming pool playing with a set of colored rubber rings that are shared by everyone at the pool. He carries the blue and red rings with him as he scampers up and down the pool steps, all the while chattering happily to himself. The green and yellow rings he has placed carefully on the edge of the pool. When another child approaches and picks up the rings, Alex wails "No! Mine!"

To the untrained eye, it appears that Alex isn't "using" those rings, and should be willing to "share." But Alex has incorporated the rings, and their placement, into his play ritual (whatever it is). He may not appear to be using the rings, but in his Two-Year-Old way, he is.

Sometimes Two-Year-Old routines have to do with the business of moving through space. Alyssa has to take the same route through the house each time. Jordan can only climb stairs while singing, "One 'tato, two 'tato . . ." as he moves up each step.

Alyssa and Jordan are not unlike an adult, getting to know a new city by car. The driver will probably take the same streets each time, until he's more familiar with the lay of the land and feels confident enough to branch out.

Indeed, Two-Year-Olds aren't alone in taking comfort from routines. We adults often find it soothing and re-assuring to have our own special chair, the little hook where we hang our keys so we won't lose them, the careful ritual of locking up the house before we go to bed. All this is practical, and it's also comforting. Like Two-Year-Olds, Mommies and Daddies sleep easier when they know that everything in their world is settled and okay.

How to Make the Most of Your Child's Love of Routine

- Take advantage of her eagerness for order to move your Two-Year-Old through her day. She'll be more agreeable to everything from putting on her mittens to washing her hands for dinner if she's used to doing things that way.
- Allow her plenty of time to do things at her own pace. If she feels rushed, she's more likely to dig in her heels.
- Accept her need for comfort rituals. If she falls asleep more easily with her special Blankie, that's fine. If she still sucks her thumb, let it be.
- Schedule her day fairly closely. Just as you engaged in household engineering to keep her safe and protect your own sanity, you need to engineer a routine that keeps everything on an even keel and gives her the comfort she craves.
- If for any reason you have to change her routine, do it gradually. For example, if you're going back to work

and you'll have to get her up and dressed earlier, see if you can change her sleep schedule ahead of time.

- Tell her ahead of time what's going to happen next. If you're going to change a routine, let her know in advance.

- Avoid head-to-head battles where possible. One father, who has steered two Two-Year-Olds on to bigger and better things, remembers his approach this way: "Instead of butting heads all the time, you kind of go along with the force. You see which direction it's going, and see if you can accommodate it. Everything doesn't have to be a big deal."

DECISIONS, DECISIONS

Last year, when your One-Year-Old wanted to assert herself, she probably did it by saying "No." This year, she can explain herself more fully. She'll insist. She'll demand. She'll resist. And there will be times when she won't be able to make up her mind what she wants.

Two-Year-Olds have more trouble making decisions than they did when they were One. They have moved from resisting everything with a resounding "No" to indecisiveness and mood swings. One moment your child will demand macaroni and cheese, and then when you're ready to serve it, she may insist on hot dogs.

This year, she benefits from being able to choose but may have trouble actually making a choice. You have to walk a fine line between running everything and deciding everything, and offering her reasonable choices just to have her freeze in indecision.

In general, you want to keep certain realms flexible

when possible. Which T-shirt she wears, or whether she has peanut butter or cheese in her sandwich, or whether you read *Goodnight Moon* or *Bedtime for Frances* are choices you can let her make.

Don't offer a choice if only one selection is acceptable (don't ask what color chalk she wants to scribble with if you've only got green!). If you do offer choices and have a preference, however, offer your preferred one last; that's the one she's more likely to choose.

You'll have to be ready, however, to lift the burden of choosing from your Two-Year-Old if she gets stuck. You'll soon learn to sense when the best thing to do is just give her peanut butter, or green chalk, without putting pressure on her to choose.

WAKING AND SLEEPING

One of your Two-Year-Old's tasks this year is learning to get herself to sleep at bedtime, and back again if she wakes during the night. She may not accomplish this task entirely this year, but she should be moving toward it.

This does not mean she's ready to toddle off to bed all by herself as she will when she's much older. She'll still need you to participate in the bedtime ritual. But after the lights are out, she may sing to herself for awhile, or talk to herself, or even whimper a bit, until she drops off. That's a sign that she is shifting the "falling-asleep" job to herself.

It's a rare Two-Year-Old who goes to bed every night with perfect tranquility, never waking or fussing or otherwise making trouble. She'll probably resist bedtime, try various stalling techniques and elaborate her bedtime rituals as much as she possibly can.

By the end of the year, however, bedtime should be easier. She will be doing a better job of getting to sleep and back to sleep on her own, and her insistence on endless hugs, stories and drinks of water should ease off.

BEDTIME: HOW TO HELP

- Try to keep bedtime to the same time every night. A regular schedule will help her feel sleepy at around the same time each night. Since she responds to sameness, you can say, "It's eight o'clock! Time for jammies."
- Don't forget to give her a friendly warning that bedtime is approaching. Transitions are harder this year, and she'll be more cooperative if she can prepare herself for the end of playtime and the beginning of bedtime. Ten minutes warning is usually enough.
- Be prepared to adjust your Two-Year-Old's bedtime to her sleep needs. She will probably sleep between nine and thirteen hours a day this year, slightly down, on average, from last year. You may need to make bedtime a bit later. However, as she eliminates her naps this year, she'll probably get sleepy earlier in the evening.
- Whatever adjustment you make, do let your Two-Year-Old know that bedtime is a serious matter and you expect her to quiet down whether she is sleepy or not.
- Avoid roughhousing or other stimulating play right before bedtime.
- Scheduling bath time right before bed usually helps a

Two-Year-Old wind down, unless your child considers bath time the height of excitement.

- Your Two-Year-Old will have her own ritual for bedtime, and as far as you reasonably can, go along with the drill. She may require her teddy, her favorite blanket, several stories, a certain light left on, the door open just so, the shades pulled down just the right amount, and three or four hugs.

- Talk about all the pleasant things you'll do tomorrow. Of course, she'll need to go to sleep in order for tomorrow to come!

- Your Two-Year-Old may want to say good night to whatever it is she collects or hoards. She may want to tuck in every one of her dolls, or say a prolonged good night to every one of her shoes, or all her books. As she collects more possessions, she may try to prolong her good-night rituals.

- Expect your Two-Year-Old to make changes in her routine as the year progresses. She may give up some of the good nights, and want to hear more about the next day's activities.

- Allow plenty of time for bedtime so you're not rushed. If you hurry, or try to cut corners, your Two-Year-Old may try to extend bedtime even longer.

- Make sure the bedtime routine has a conclusion. Especially at midyear, your Two-Year-Old may try to extend the ritual beyond reason. Follow her lead in determining exactly what the end is—the final hug, the final good night—and make that stick. If you have trouble concluding the process, set a kitchen timer for five to ten minutes. When the bell rings, bedtime is over.

- A clock radio, set to play on a soothing station for a short period of time, may help your Two-Year-Old ease into sleep. A quiet story tape may help, as well.
- If you travel, or if there has been a disruption in your life, do your best to retain your child's going-to-bed ritual.

WAKEFULNESS: HOW TO HELP

- If your Two-Year-Old cries or whimpers during the night, don't be too quick to go to her. She may just be half-awake and able to settle on her own.
- On the other hand, do respond if she seems genuinely distressed. Her pajamas may be tangled, or she may be thirsty or frightened.
- Respond to nightmares quickly and soothingly.
- If your Two-Year-Old gets out of bed during the night, return her to bed or crib calmly, but firmly. Do not play with her, read to her, or be more interesting than bed. In fact, try to be as boring as possible.
- Make sure she's getting enough of your attention during the day.
- If you're concerned about her wandering during the night while you're sleeping, you may need to keep a gate across her door.
- Your Two-Year-Old is growing more amenable to reason every day. Remind her that she is big enough to stay in bed, and that's what you expect her to do.
- Consider giving her a small reward in the morning when she stays in bed all night.

NAP TIME: HOW TO HELP

Your Two-Year-Old has probably cut back to one nap by this year, and she may well eliminate naps altogether. If she does this, you will probably want to continue with a "play nap" during which she isn't expected to sleep, but can rest and play quietly.

- If your Two-Year-Old resists going off to bed for nap time, allow her to nap in a special place, like a sleeping bag in a corner of the family room.
- Watch for signs of fatigue and try to get her to nap before she's totally exhausted and out of sorts.
- Use a much shorter version of the bedtime routine to settle your child down for a nap.
- Don't let your Two-Year-Old sleep too long during a nap, or she won't be sleepy at bedtime.
- Lots of Twos are cranky when they first awaken from a nap. Allow her some warm-up time between when she wakes up and when you have to rush her into some activity.
- If your child is shifting from a sleep nap to a play nap, treat it as a continuation of the nap routine she's used to. She'll be less likely to resist. You want her to take a break, because both you and she get tired during the day and need a rest.

IN THE MORNING: HOW TO HELP

- If you want your Two-Year-Old to sleep a bit longer

(and who doesn't!), try using room-darkening window shades.

- Your child will probably play or chatter to herself when she first wakes up. If she is still in a crib, she will probably call out to you; if you call back in a friendly manner, you may be able to stall her and get a few minutes more sleep.

- As she gets closer to Three, she should be able to play for awhile in her room before coming to wake you up. You can encourage this by leaving toys in her crib or bed after she is asleep for the night, or leaving a small cup of juice on a table near her bed.

- You may want to allow your Two-Year-Old to join you in bed when she wakes up. Just make sure that it really is morning—otherwise she may get in the habit of appearing in your bedroom at midnight.

DRESSING

At Two, your child will probably need considerable help in getting dressed, but she'll show quite a bit of interest in managing her clothes herself. By mid-year, she may not accept your help. The more she is able to do things for herself without becoming hopelessly frustrated, the better.

Remember, toddlers usually learn to undress before they dress. They'll unbutton and unzip before they can button and zip. Your Two-Year-Old will be empowered by the experience of removing her clothing, and may cheerfully show up with nothing on at all.

However, this year, she will acquire many dressing skills, along with a growing desire to behave in a grown-up manner. Wherever possible, encourage her growing ability to take care of herself.

How to Help

- Keep clothing simple and suited to Two-Year-Old activities. Avoid frilly garments that get in the way. Save the ruffly dresses and the adorable sailor suits for holidays and portrait time.
- Provide loose-fitting clothing with simple closures like big zippers, or none at all (elastic-waist pants are simplest).
- Allow your child to choose her clothing. If there are three clean T-shirts in the drawer, let her choose which one to put on.
- Give her plenty of time for dressing.
- Teach her specific skills, like pulling on a shoe or pushing a button through a buttonhole, by starting the task yourself and then saying, "Now you can do the rest." Gradually leave more and more for her to do.

BATHING

Your Two-Year-Old will probably enjoy bath time at least as much as she did last year. And while you may have trouble getting her into the tub, you'll probably have as much trouble getting her out.

Most Twos accept the washing and drying of hands as part of their routine. A stool next to the sink will help her learn to handle this skill independently.

Your Two-Year-Old may still resist having her face

washed. She may be willing if you give her a damp washcloth and let her wash herself. You can always touch up afterward.

TEETH

During this year, the percentage of children with tooth decay rises from eight to nearly sixty, so it's important to have your child see a dentist. If she visits a dentist for a simple checkup, and nothing has to be done to her teeth, she will be less likely to fear visits to the dentist later on.

This is also the time to incorporate regular brushing into your child's routines. If she has her own colorful toothbrush and sees other family members brushing their own teeth, she will be eager to participate.

Give your Two-Year-Old a soft-bristle brush, and use either no toothpaste at all or very little (she is not likely to understand rinsing and spitting, and is likely to swallow her toothpaste). At first, she will probably brush her face as much as her teeth, and will not do an adequate brushing job on her own. But it's important to let her begin, and then finish the process yourself.

If you start her on a toothbrushing routine now, and get her accustomed to making it part of her bedtime ritual, chances are she will learn to care for her own teeth in good time.

TOILETING

When you had a One-Year-Old, perfect strangers wanted to know when your little darling learned to walk.

This year, everybody seems to want to know if your Two-Year-Old is out of diapers, or when she will be. The whole world seems to have a stake in toilet training, whether it's your in-laws, the preschool where you want to send your child next month, or just that helpful stranger on a park bench next to you.

It's easy to get stressed about toileting, because as a parent burdened by diaper duty, you probably can't wait until your child reaches this particular milestone.

But the chances are that the less you worry, the more smoothly things will progress. Studies have indicated that the earlier you start, the longer the process takes, and the more frustrating it is for all concerned. So it's probably best to make sure you have seen signs of true readiness in your child before you begin.

Readiness

You can't rush Mother Nature. Babies can't control their elimination; toddlers are just beginning to be able to, and even for many Three-Year-Olds, bowel and bladder control is an inexact science.

Sometime during the first half of this year, most Two-Year-Olds' bodies become more regulated in many functions, including elimination. Their bowels move more or less at the same time of day, and they can retain urine for longer periods of time. At twenty-four months, they may be able to stay dry for an hour or two; by later in the year, they may go four or five hours between wet diapers. This process can't be hurried; the sphincter muscles in the anus and urethra must be mature enough to be opened and closed at will. Also, the child needs to develop enough control to retain urine voluntarily when her bladder is full.

However, physical readiness is not enough. Your child will need to be emotionally and intellectually ready before all systems are go. Often, a child who was co-operative at twenty-five months (but not physically ready) is more physically mature at twenty-eight months, but not in the mood to do much of anything that Mommy and Daddy want.

There's a great deal of variation in when children signal readiness for toilet learning. In general, girls are ready a bit sooner than boys. For many children, all these factors come together around Two-and-a-Half. However, even children who learn at that point often have accidents until they're Three.

Usually, your Two-Year-Old will signal her readiness by:

- Showing discomfort or distress at being wet or soiled.
- Showing awareness of an imminent bowel movement or urination. She will be aware during and after the fact first; later she'll show that she is anticipating the event. She won't be able to make good use of the toilet or potty chair until she can anticipate.
- Showing an interest in the way adults use the toilet, and an interest in being more grown-up.
- Being able to stay dry for two hours.

Bowel Vs. Bladder Control

For many children, bowel and bladder control come at pretty much the same time. Still, bowel control is easier to master than bladder control, and often precedes it.

- Bowel movements occur fewer times per day.
- They require a conscious effort on the part of the child.
- There's usually plenty of warning to a helpful adult (your child may turn red, or show signs of straining).
- The time between the first warning sign and the movement is long enough to get the child to the potty.

Your child's ability to control urination, on the other hand, is more difficult. She has to be able to sense when her bladder is full, and be able to retain urine until she can reach a toilet.

How to Help

- Accept the fact that toilet learning is one more area of development where there is a great deal of variation, and much of it is unexplained. So don't fret, don't compare, and most of all, don't convey impatience or disappointment to your child.
- If you haven't already introduced her to a potty chair, you can do so even before she's ready. Let her try sitting on it, even in diapers, just to get comfortable with it.
- Tell her what it's for, and explain that when she's bigger and ready to give up diapers, she'll use that. And soon after that she'll be able to use the big toilet like Mommy and Daddy (or brothers and sisters).
- When you think she's ready, pick a time when she can scamper around without diapers or pants (in the sum-

mer, in the backyard, for example). That way, she can easily get to the potty when she needs to, but any mistakes will be of little consequence.

- Prior to this training session, give her extra liquids.
- Praise success, but don't overdo it. If you're over-eager, it makes toilet learning into an issue of pleasing Mommy and Daddy, rather than an issue of growing up and being more independent.
- Once she does start using the regular toilet, don't scare her with sudden flushing. Many children find that distressing.
- While she's learning, reserve diapers for nighttime use and special occasions, like trips. Once she's out of diapers most of the time, it's best not to switch back and forth. If you do, she'll have to stop and think if she is wearing a diaper or not.
- When your child is newly trained and wearing pants, remind yourself to take her to the bathroom regularly. It's easy to forget, since you've been thinking in terms of diapers all these years. Once the diaper safety net is gone, you have to be more vigilant. The more you help her remember (and remember for her), the more success she'll experience.
- However, don't nag. Soon, she'll have to take over the job of remembering.
- Never punish accidents. As you help your child clean up after a failure, refer to her disappointment, not your own: "That's too bad, honey. You'll remember next time."

As Different As Day and Night

Even if your Two-Year-Old gets the hang of using the toilet during the day this year, staying dry at night may take quite a bit longer. Before about Two-and-a-Half, most children wake up wet. Quite a few accomplish nighttime dryness by their Third birthday, but many do not reach that point until quite a bit later (often not until age Five).

After all, to stay dry all through the night, your child has to learn all the elements of daytime control, and she has to manage this while fast asleep. This is a process that can't be rushed. Even if you wanted to, you can't "teach" her when she's fast asleep.

If your child is consistently dry on wakening, however, you might want to let her try sleeping without a diaper. Here are some suggestions if you try this.

- Keep the process calm and low-pressure, just as you did with daytime training.
- Wait until she is sleeping in a regular bed, or can safely and easily get out of her crib to go to the bathroom on her own.
- Put a plastic sheet under her regular cloth sheet. Explain to her that it's there just in case she wets, and if that happens it's okay.
- Take her to the bathroom just before bed.
- Use training pants and plastic pants, at least at the beginning of the process.
- Each time she wakes dry, praise her for her accomplishment.

MAKING HERSELF USEFUL

This year, while your Two-Year-Old is eager to help and fond of routines, is an ideal time to introduce her to being a good helper. Even though her "help" may make everything take longer, and be messier, she can still:

- Set out a spoon for Mommy, a spoon for Daddy, and a spoon for herself at mealtime.
- Tear lettuce leaves for salad.
- Mix batter.
- Put dirty clothes in the hamper.
- Pick tomatoes (if you remind her not to pick the green ones!).
- Fetch things for you (the TV schedule, a napkin or tissue).
- Bring in the newspaper.

When she does these things, be sure to thank her graciously.

TIME CAPSULES
24 Months

At Two, your child is probably reasonably cooperative about her daily routines. She can put on some garments, but lets you handle the rest. She may express a dislike of dirty hands, clothes, or diapers. She may be able to stay dry during the day for several hours. She can turn on water faucets and wash and dry her hands. She may begin brushing her teeth. She handles a spoon and cup fairly well at mealtime. She probably takes only one nap. She resists bedtime and tries to draw out her going-to-sleep routines.

30 Months

At this stage, your Two-Year-Old's rigidity increases. She dislikes any change in her routine. She may show physical signs of readiness for toileting but be resistant. She may go for four hours without urinating. She is getting better at dressing herself, but may fight and squirm when you try to help. She is more adept at eating, and can handle a fork. She may stop taking naps altogether, but she'll still need a quiet session or play nap.

36 Months

By the end of the year, your Two-Year-Old has moved through her most rigid period. She is becoming more confident and relaxed in many areas, including bedtime and toileting. She may well have achieved daytime control by now, and many Threes are ready for nighttime control. She is less resistant at bedtime, and her routine can be streamlined somewhat.

QUESTIONS AND ANSWERS

Q: *My son is almost Three and still refuses to give up diapers, and he's outgrowing the largest size they make! We're just about ready to give up. We can tell* *when he's about to have a bowel movement, but when we ask him, he insists that he's not. What should we do?*

A: Patience is a virtue. He is clearly able to understand what is happening physically, and he probably understands what you want him to do. He is not quite ready to give up the comforts of the old way. He will take that step sooner if you try not to hover.

Perhaps it would be better if you don't try to get him to change horses in midstream. Sometime when he is not having a bowel movement, bring up the subject of being more grown-up by using the toilet. Tell him that you know he'll be able to manage soon. Then let him do things his way for awhile.

Q: *My daughter still insists on a pacifier when she goes to bed. She never uses it anywhere else. Now that she's Two, shouldn't I try to get her to stop?*

A: Last year, your daughter still had a need to suck, and the pacifier served that need. This year, her need for sucking is less, but her need for comfort during times of transitions is still great. The pacifier represents everything that has given her comfort during her life: food, Mommy, familiar things. Right now, she is learning the mechanics of falling asleep, and falling back to sleep when she wakes at night, and to do these things without involving you too much.

Her pacifier helps her do these thing. She won't need it forever, so your best bet this year is to allow her her little crutch.

Q: *Ordinarily, our thirty-three-month-old son sleeps through the night quite well, but when he has a scary dream he insists on coming into bed with us. My husband thinks if we let him do this, he'll want to sleep with us all the time. Should we permit it?*

A: Any scary experience—whether external, like thunderstorms, or internal, like nightmares—is bound to interfere with a Two-Year-Old's ability to fall back to sleep. If he is genuinely frightened, he needs your comfort, and it's probably worth the inconvenience of having him come to your room if it eases his fears. You don't want to leave him frightened and alone, just to uphold the letter of the law. Alternately, you could sit with him in his own room until he falls back to sleep.

Your husband's concern is that your son may take advantage of the situation and claim nightmares just so he can sleep with you. The key is to determine what your child is seeking: If he is genuinely frightened, provide comfort; if he is seeking companionship at 2 A.M., do not provide it, but insist calmly that he return to his own bed.

9

Refined Tastes:
Food and Nutrition

When Megan turned Two, she abruptly stopped eating chicken and potatoes. Megan's parents, who like chicken and potatoes and serve one or both quite often, were puzzled. They tried preparing these items in numerous tempting ways, but Megan still refused. When they asked her why she didn't want her chicken, she just said, "Don't like it."

Having just survived a year of Megan's One-Year-Old fussiness, they finally concluded that she was going through another of her quirks, and gave up on chicken and potatoes.

The burning question now is, will Megan eventually come around? That depends on whether she is experiencing a temporary bout of fussiness, as she often did last year, or if she is simply developing her own preferences in food.

By age Two, your child knows what he likes. He is developing his own unique tastes, just as you have yours. If you dislike anything with garlic and find your host is serving pasta with pesto sauce at a dinner party, probably your heart sinks (although as an adult, you will probably make the best of it).

In your own home, you can choose whatever you want to prepare and avoid what you don't like. Your Two-Year-Old can't do that, so you'll have to strike a compromise that honors his individuality but doesn't deprive other family members. After all, it's hard to feed a family if you can never, ever serve chicken or potatoes.

Your Two-Year-Old will probably continue to have an inconsistent appetite, as he did last year, and you may wonder if he is eating enough. He will continue to go on food jags, wanting nothing but macaroni and cantaloupe for days on end.

But by the time he is Three, he will be well past the worst of his fussy eating days. His appetite will improve somewhat, and he will be more willing to try new foods because he will be past the worst of the contrary stage he'll have at midyear.

He will also be much more adept at feeding himself and being a reasonably civilized dining companion. He will improve his skills with spoon, fork, and cup. He will chew better, spill less. He will learn the rudiments of simple table manners.

Also this year, your Two-Year-Old will continue to learn what real food tastes like, and he'll develop tastes that will last him a lifetime. That's one reason, aside from direct nutritional reasons, why you want him to enjoy the flavor of plain oatmeal, fresh strawberries, good whole-wheat bread, lean meats, and why you'll want to shield him, as much as you reasonably can, from sweetened cereals and candy and soda.

MEALTIME: ONE MORE ROUTINE

Mealtime serves to nourish more than your child's body. A fairly regular schedule of meals and snacks is another dimension of the way his whole life is made up of routines. Just as he will get sleepy at the same time each night, his stomach will remind him of mealtime in a predictable way. He'll learn that lunchtime means washing and drying his hands, making a few choices about sandwich fillings or which cup to use, and then enjoying a meal.

Of course, as with all routines, his feeding schedule should not be inflexible. You don't have to force a hungry child to wait, or an unhungry one to eat, just to be consistent. All is not lost just because Saturday was so hectic that nobody had a proper breakfast, or if your Two-Year-Old discovered the dessert table at a picnic and filled up too much to eat his hamburger.

Because your Two-Year-Old loves having everything the same, this year will probably mark the high point of demands for the same food day after day. These food jags will recede on their own, as will your Two-Year-Old's rigidity.

How to Help

• Keep it simple. Two-Year-Old tastes, and Two-Year-Old tolerance for delay and formality are quite limited. Save your gourmet efforts for adults meals. The more

171

work you put into the preparation of food, you can bet the less your child will seem to appreciate it.

• Make it quick. Don't make a hungry Two-Year-Old sit waiting and waiting while you fuss to make his lunch just perfect.

• Serve small quantities. Children who are light eaters anyway will feel daunted by large portions.

• Recognize, and work with, your child's hunger schedule. Some toddlers enjoy a hearty breakfast and eat lightly the rest of the day; others don't build up an appetite until later in the day.

• Be tolerant of fingers. Two-Year-Olds will make progress in the use of utensils this year, but most will still use fingers, at least for some foods. If your child eats well, be grateful and don't be too concerned about how the food got from plate to mouth.

WHY YOUR TWO-YEAR-OLD "DOESN'T EAT"

After the rapid pace of his first twelve months, your child's growth rate slowed down last year. That slow growth continues this year, and with it, his fairly modest appetite. If your Two-Year-Old is healthy and has been growing normally, he has been getting enough to eat. Studies have shown that if toddlers are offered a variety of foods, without pressure, they will select—over time—a fairly balanced diet. At any one meal, however, or on any one day, it may not seem balanced at all.

However, this year he is learning to assert himself, and resist you, with more vigor. One of his simplest techniques is to refuse to eat, or to refuse a certain kind of food. Your chances of forcing him to eat the way you want are not good this year, so you'll be better off letting him skip a meal and experience hunger as a result, rather than getting into a huge battle of wills.

FOOD AS POWER

Food is more than food. From the lover's candlelit dinner to the prisoner's last meal, food is tied up with the intricacies of culture, social relationships, passions, rewards and punishments. Within families, it's all complicated by the money we spent to buy the food, the work we did to prepare it, the sin of wasting perfectly good food, and our eagerness to see our children grow and thrive.

When your child was a baby, food was a simple pleasure that mother and father provided. Last year, he learned to provide some of it himself, with his fingers or sometimes with a spoon. That gave him a feeling of power and autonomy, along with the pleasure of a tasty meal. Then he began to learn that his eating satisfied his parents as well, and not eating displeased them.

"Just one more bite, sweetie. Please? Just one more bite for Mommy?"

"Look at that boy! He cleaned his plate. Good boy!"

"Eat all your meat, dear, so you'll grow up big and strong."

"No ice cream for you until you eat those vegetables!"

The familiar refrains of toddler mealtime revolve around how very much we want them to eat, how important it is to us.

So we wheedle, we bribe, we beg, we measure, we

knit our brows and wring our hands. Suddenly the balance of power has shifted. The Two-Year-Old is the gatekeeper, and we are the supplicants who want very much to get it open.

Maybe it will open for blueberry yogurt, and only blueberry yogurt. Maybe it won't open at all. For many a One- and Two-Year-Old, that sense of control is so appealing that it's worth missing a meal or two.

How to Help

- Accept that your child may not eat as much as you might think he should. You do want to encourage him by making mealtime as pleasant as possible, and by offering appealing food. But let him be the arbiter of how much he wants.
- Do not pressure, force, coax, or bribe him to eat more than he wants.
- Serve food in small amounts, with seconds available. This has two advantages: He won't be overwhelmed by small portions, and you won't get anxious about wasting "perfectly good food" if he doesn't finish.
- Do not bribe him with the promise of treats. Right now, he is interested in food for its own sake; there's no need to rush him into the world of candy and sweets as a reward.
- Separate food issues, which have to do with nourishment, from discipline issues. Keep reward and punishment away from the kitchen table.
- If he refuses to eat and you think he is doing it to resist you, let him experience the logical consequence of not eating: hunger. If he asks for food ten minutes

after lunch, say, "I know you must feel pretty hungry. But lunch is over. You'll have to wait for snack time." Do not relent and feed him ahead of schedule if he's refused a meal.

• Offer new foods but don't make too much of them. Present a small amount of the new food in a matter-of-fact way and let him decide whether to taste it. Don't pressure him to take "just one bite." Be patient. He may need to see the new food many times before he feels ready to try it.

• One way to offer a new food to a Two-Year-Old is to serve it just to the adults and wait for the child's curiosity to kick in. "Oh boy," says Daddy. "Pass me some of that eggplant." Chances are, after a few experiences of Daddy enjoying eggplant, your Two-Year-Old will say "I want some!" At this point, give him just a taste and don't fret if he rejects it this time.

• If he suddenly rejects tomatoes and you know he used to love tomatoes, respect his wishes. Wait a week or so, then offer them again.

PREVENTING LIFELONG EATING PROBLEMS

During these preschool years, it's important that your child receive adequate nourishment. But it's also important that he develop eating habits that will serve him well the rest of his life. Many of these patterns are established by age Three, and bad habits are much harder to alter after that.

If your Two-Year-Old is fussy about food, it won't do much lasting harm. But if you turn food into a battleground, getting the simple act of eating all tangled up with displine and love and the withholding of love, your child may develop poor habits.

Those poor habits can be avoided. You don't have to make it harder on yourself and your child by being drawn into an emotional contest of wills. For some parents, that battle is with the fussy eater himself. For others, it's a battle with Grandma, who makes them feel inadequate because "He eats so little! Are you sure you're feeding him enough?"

Adults who eat for comfort, who crave only junk food, who despise vegetables, who overeat or starve themselves, can probably trace their unhealthful habits to their earliest toddler years.

What happens is that food becomes separated from its biological function of providing fuel and satisfaction. Infants cry when they are hungry, and, when fed, eat until they are full. Then they stop. But toddlers whose parents succeed in stuffing them when they are not hungry may develop a habit of eating long after hunger has been satisfied.

So pressuring toddlers to eat is counterproductive on two counts: If you succeed in getting your child to eat more than he wants, he may develop a habit of overeating; and if you fail, he may actually eat less than he wants just to resist you.

If you can manage to keep food to the simple dimensions it had in his infancy, you will be well on the way to avoiding eating problems later, not to mention parent-toddler battles in the here and now.

When we discussed setting limits in Chapter 7, we suggested examining your own feelings about rules and punishments. The realm of food is also full of risk for parent-toddler conflict. It may be wise to examine your own feelings about feeding. Were you raised to clean your plate at all costs? Are you determined not to feed your toddler the soda and junk food you were permitted? Were you raised with a horror of ever wasting food? Your own experience colors your own hopes and fears for your child. Give some thought to the agenda you bring to the kitchen table.

TYPICAL TWO-YEAR-OLD QUIRKS

Gavin's family loves to garden, and Gavin has always been a good consumer of green vegetables. But when he turned two, he suddenly refused to eat green beans— unless they were whole. He would happily consume green beans if they were served as nature made them. But he would refuse to touch them if they were cut up, or, as he called them, "broken."

An aversion to food in certain forms is common among Two-Year-Olds, along with other quirks:

- Two-Year-Olds may still hate to have one kind of food touch another. If this is the case, continue to use a divided baby plate or serve courses on separate dishes.
- Texture is important. Your toddler may accept boiled potatoes or french fries, but not mashed. He may reject asparagus, not for flavor but for texture. He may reject cooked vegetables in general, but accept crisp fresh ones.
- Sauces and gravies are usually not well received. Adults may prefer their vegetables drenched in cheese sauce; your Two-Year-Old may be more willing to accept them straight up.

If you accommodate your child's preferences and tastes this year, you will probably find that most of these quirks fade as your child approaches Three.

A WORD ABOUT TABLE MANNERS

It will be quite some time before you can comfortably take your Two-Year-Old to Buckingham Palace for tea. However, he is much more able this year than last to learn some rudiments of mealtime civility.

- Do have some "formal" meals together so he can practice his skills. Use a tablecloth and (perhaps) the good china. He may well rise to the occasion.
- Even if he's not the best dinner companion, do let him join you at family meals at least some of the time. He needs to see how adults eat and behave at the table.
- Remember your own manners on these occasions. Say "please" and "thank you" to him, as well as to your spouse.
- Don't demand that he use these polite words, but praise him generously when he does.
- Even Twos who are doing their best at mealtime have a hard time sitting through a long meal waiting until everyone has finished. Forcing a squirmy Two-Year-Old to wait can make mealtime miserable for all concerned, so it's probably best this year to let him leave the table when he becomes restless.
- If the family is eating together and he is totally disruptive, remove him and his plate from the table and to a neutral spot. Don't punish him. Soon he'll get the

message that if he acts like a big boy, he can sit with the family.

Generally, formal restaurants and Two-Year-Olds do not mix well, although many Twos can do quite well at a family-oriented eatery where the atmosphere is informal.

Some families, however, have more success than others taking small children to fairly elegant restaurants. Here's what a father of three preschoolers has to say:

"Our policy is to prepare for the worst and expect the best, and the best is what we usually get. We have restaurant rules, and we always prepare the kids ahead of time by reminding them of how a restaurant is different from home. We remind them to use their 'restaurant voice,' for example. Of course that works better with the older ones, but Zach's getting better all the time.

"We bring quiet toys, paper and crayons, so they have something to do before the food comes. Usually we'll just order an appetizer or a bowl of soup for Zach. We bring packaged crackers, unless we know the restaurant has breadsticks for them to munch on while they wait. If one of our kids does get out of hand, my wife or I takes them out immediately. But that hardly ever happens. We've had compliments from complete strangers on the way our children behave, and my wife and I have the advantage of being able to enjoy decent restaurants without having to get a sitter."

WHAT YOUR TWO-YEAR-OLD NEEDS TO EAT

Now that we've established how you can avoid the most common feeding problems that crop up this year, what foods should you offer your Two-Year-Old? Your child's food intake will probably be only slightly higher than it was when he was One. The major differences this year: His improved chewing ability widens the variety of foods he can eat, and, at Two, he can switch from whole to low-fat milk. Eventually, he will benefit from drinking skim milk; experts disagree on whether to make the switch abruptly at Two or work your way down through 2 percent and 1 percent. Your pediatrician can guide you.

- Milk and milk products. A pint of milk per day should fulfill his calcium requirement and provide protein and minerals as well. Your child also gets calcium from cheese (chunks, slices, or crumbled), preferably fairly mild and preferably unprocessed; yogurt, and occasional frozen yogurt or ice cream.
- Several servings (totaling four or five ounces daily) of meat or high protein equivalent, like eggs, beans or cheese. You'll still need to cut meat for him. He may be able to manage a chicken drumstick if you're careful about any sharp bones. Eggs can be served scrambled, or hard boiled and cut up.

Cheese is often very popular this year. Some children dislike the texture of cottage cheese and the strong flavor of Swiss and sharp Cheddar. Try mild cheeses such as Monterey jack, ricotta, Colby. And don't forget string cheese, an enjoyable finger food.

Hot dogs are popular with toddlers; but be warned that they can still be a choking hazard in Two-Year-Olds. Cut hot dogs in pieces, or slice lengthwise twice before serving on a bun. Try to keep your Two-Year-

Old's consumption of hot dogs to a reasonable minimum, because they tend to be high in fat and additives.

- Four or more servings of fruits and vegetables. Vegetables are often rejected this year; if they are, increase the servings of fruit. Don't be surprised if your Two-Year-Old rejects spinach, asparagus, and vegetables with a bitter taste.

  Fruits can be fresh or stewed; vegetables fresh or cooked. Try steaming vegetables to retain crispness and color and prevent the dreaded sogginess.

  Grapes and cherries can be a choking hazard; cut them in half (and remove all seeds and stones!). If your Two-Year-Old still has trouble with the stringy membrane on orange segments, remove them.

- Breads, grains, and potatoes. Four or more servings, with half a slice of bread, half a muffin, or about a quarter cup of cooked cereal counting as a serving. Include a variety of breads, with the emphasis on whole wheat and other whole grains. Offer muffins, whole-wheat crackers, bagels, tortillas, pita bread, potatoes, cooked noodles, spaghetti or other pasta, and rice.

  Oatmeal, Wheatena, and Cream of Wheat and Rice are fine. Don't put sugar on your toddler's cereal (if you don't start, he won't miss it). Avoid sweetened cereals.

- Fluids, such as unsweetened fruit juice or plain water. Apple juice is a staple beverage, but recent studies have warned against offering toddlers unlimited amounts because it can take the place of milk or other foods.

HOW NOT TO SHARPEN A SWEET TOOTH

A preference for sweet flavors seems to be inborn in humans. If you tempt your child with candy, cookies, doughnuts, and soda, he'll probably yield to temptation. But sweet treats will fill him up and replace the food he needs, just when he's fussy at mealtimes anyway.

During this year, your child is continuing to establish his food and flavor preferences. If he becomes accustomed to intensely sweetened foods, he'll lean toward those in later life. Right now, he needs to learn about and appreciate the fruity sweetness of fresh peaches, and the subtle, nutty sweetness of plain oatmeal. He needs to think of real food as tasty and satisfying.

The same holds true for added salt. The last thing you want to establish this year is a craving for highly salted snack foods.

When your child starts school, and spends more time among other children, it will be much harder to limit sweets. But right now, you do have the advantage. You can't make him eat, but you can determine the menu of foods you offer him.

The occasional sweet treat ought not to harm your Two-Year-Old, especially if it's just viewed as something that tastes good, rather than a powerful talisman of parental disapproval, or reward and comfort.

FOODS TO AVOID

Two-Year-Olds have trouble chewing and swallowing foods that are otherwise acceptable for older children. Avoid the following:

- Peanuts; which can be inhaled by toddlers and even preschoolers.
- Large, stringy orange slices (remove membranes and offer in small pieces).
- Popcorn.
- Hard candies.
- Raisins.
- Sunflower seeds.
- Whole grapes and cherries, and anything with pits.

QUESTIONS AND ANSWERS

Q: *How can I get my son to eat vegetables? I know how important it is, nutritionally, to include more vegetables. But he absolutely refuses. He hates anything green.*

A: Many toddlers dislike the flavor of green vegetables, especially the bitter ones, such as spinach and Brussels sprouts. They are more likely to accept the mild-flavored ones—peas, squash, and green beans, for example.

Consider vegetable soup, either homemade or commercial. You can pour the broth into a cup for drinking, and let him pick up the other pieces with his spoon or fingers. And try vegetable juice, as well.

If you can get away with it, incorporate vegetables into other foods he'll eat. Bits of broccoli or spinach may be acceptable in an omelet or a stew.

Finally, don't force the issue. If your son is adamant about vegetables, just ease up and offer more fruit.

Q: *My sister-in-law feeds her kids soda, candy, and all kinds of foods that we never have in our house. What should I do when she offers our daughter these things?*

A: It's not always easy to do so graciously, but you should try to limit your daughter's exposure to these foods when you can. The time will come soon enough when you won't be able to control what she eats. When the situation you describe arises, your best bet is simply to tell your host, "Sorry, but Samantha doesn't eat (whatever)." Most people will accept the idea that Two-Year-Olds have somewhat limited diets, and either can't or won't eat everything.

If you know you're going to be in a home where there's not likely to be any juice or wholesome snacks, take your own supplies along.

Q: *We do try to have family meals, but how can we do this when our Two-Year-Old hates so many things? It doesn't seem reasonable that we can never have fish as a family meal because our daughter refuses to eat fish.*

A: First of all, go ahead and serve fish when you feel like. it. A Two-Year-Old doesn't have to hold the rest of the family's meals hostage to her own preferences.

Once fish is on the menu, however, you have several options, depending on how much of an issue you want to make of her eating habits.

First, you can give her a choice of having fish as the entree or nothing. If she chooses nothing, which she probably will, she could have additional servings of potatoes or vegetables or bread, to fill up.

Or you can provide her with a substitute. The rest of you can have fish, and she can have an hard-boiled egg or a piece of cheese.

Or you can prepare a new kind of fish, in a new way, and see if she'll accept a small amount (don't tell her it's fish; tell her it's "sole" or "salmon").

Your Two-Year-Old has a right to dislike fish, just as you probably dislike certain foods. You need to accept her developing preferences in food, but those preferences should not tyrannize the rest of the family.

10

✻

Safe and Sound:
Keeping Your Two-Year-Old
from Harm

Your Two-Year-Old is learning to remember rules, to think about causes and effects and to think ahead a bit. All these abilities will help her learn about keeping safe, but her ability to be responsible for her own safety is still a long way off. This year, as last, the burden of keeping her safe falls on you.

Certainly it's easier than it was. She is less likely than last year to pull a pan of hot food off the stove (but that doesn't mean she won't). She is less likely to put small objects in her mouth and choke (but that doesn't mean she won't).

Your task this year is to maintain the vigilance you've kept since she was a baby, remembering to update it from time to time as her strength and her curiosity increase. All the while, you'll be teaching and reinforcing safety rules and habits.

In some ways, her growing maturity can constitute a danger. She is more careful, more thoughtful than last year, and you may be lulled into thinking she is more mature than she really is.

"I couldn't believe she would do that," recalls Tori's mother. At thirty-four months, Tori, a bright, well-behaved little girl, got chewing gum in her hair. Her mother tried to get the residue out with rubbing alcohol, and set the bottle down on the kitchen table as she tried to rub off the gum. In a jiffy, Tori picked up the bottle and took a sizable swig. "I was so shocked," said her mother. "I thought she knew better. And it must have tasted awful!"

There's another challenge to keeping your Two-Year-Old safe. This year, she is more coordinated than last, but she is also bigger, stronger, and capable of more. She can open doors and jars and bottles she couldn't last year, she can climb higher, and she can run faster.

"I've noticed we're getting more accidents and bigger goose eggs than last year," one mother said of her son and his play-group friends. "They're more daring. The other day we had five skinned knees, a splinter, and a couple of bruised fingers from the swing chain."

It's probably not possible, or even advisable, to protect a Two-Year-old from all possible scrapes and bumps. But you'll certainly want to minimize the chances of injury—major or minor—for your child. This year, the best approach is a combination of supervision, careful childproofing, and the teaching of safety habits and rules.

Of these three elements, the first two are the most reliable ways of keeping your child safe. Childproofing alone can, according to one study, prevent as many as 90 percent of serious injuries that toddlers suffer in the home.

Yet this is a prime year for learning about acceptable behavior, and your Two-Year-Old will probably show interest in safety routines. She may watch you like a hawk and reprimand you if you forget to screw the child-proof cap back on the vitamin bottle, or if the fire in the fireplace isn't completely extinguished.

So by all means teach safety, and make her understand that safety rules are the most important rules of all. But you can't count on her compliance. Relying on the rules is one thing when the stakes are a stolen cookie before dinner, or muddy footprints on the good living room couch. It's another thing entirely when the stakes are your child's life and limb. She has a love-hate relationship with rules this year, and she may challenge, evade, or simply forget them.

If you're Two, and your ball rolls down the driveway into the street, you think about the ball and the fun of getting it back. You don't think about abstractions like speeding cars. You're drawn to everything, curious about everything. You remember where things are hidden now, and you remember how things are used— Dad's shaver, the one you saw him use this morning; Mom's curling iron, the one that she uses just like this on her hair . . . and Uncle Dave's cigarette lighter. And outside, the glorious swimming pool where you had such a good time yesterday beckons.

In some ways, a Two-Year-Old's temptations are greater than those of a One-Year-Old because she can remember and imitate.

Your task of keeping your Two-Year-Old safe will depend, in part, on a sixth sense you'll develop about what she's most likely to be attracted by. But a close examination and clean sweep of your home can greatly reduce hazards and increase her chances of staying safe.

YOUR CHILD'S ROOM

- If your Two-Year-Old still sleeps in a crib, make sure it's safe and still meets her needs now that she's bigger and able to move around more easily.

  First, be sure the crib meets government safety standards. The space between side slats must be no wider than 2⅜ inches. Corner posts must not be higher than the end boards, because clothing can snag on posts and cause strangulation. The ends should not have decorative cutouts. The latches used to drop the crib sides should be hard for a child to reach and operate.

  The mattress should fit snugly in the crib. This year, the mattress should be at the lowest level. Once your child can climb or fall out of the crib, it's advisable to move her to a bed.

  Place the crib far from windows and drapery pulls.

  If you move your toddler from crib to bed this year, use side rails on the bed. It takes time to get used to a real bed and not fall out.

- Keep windows locked. Open double-hung windows from the top only. You may want to install a window latch that limits how far the window will open, or—especially if your child's bedroom is above the ground floor—consider installing window guards as required by law in some cities. Do not trust screens to keep your child from falling out; some, especially on newer windows, are not made to withstand pressure and could be pushed out by a toddler.

- Avoid long curtain and drapery cords. If you do have blinds, don't let the cord hang where your toddler can reach it. Cut it as short as possible, and wind it around a cleat that's positioned out of reach.
- Mount Tot Finder decals on your child's window to make the room easy for firefighters to locate in a fire.
- If the bedroom doorknob has a locking mechanism, change the knob or reverse it, to prevent your child locking herself inside.
- Do what you can to hide, cover, disconnect, or otherwise shield electrical outlets, even if by now you think your Two-Year-Old "knows better" than to poke things into them. Where possible, move furniture in front of outlets. Get outlet covers and check regularly to make sure they're still in place.
- Toy chests, especially older ones, can be a hazard: Children can get inside and pull the lid closed; hinges can pinch tiny fingers; lids can slam down on fingers or heads.

  If you must use one, make sure it is either ventilated or too small for your child to climb into. Glue wooden blocks on the corners, so that when the lid closes, it won't pinch fingers. Better yet, store toys on open shelves or in cubbies instead.
- You'll still need to keep one hand on your squirmer when you've got her on her changing table.
- Avoid talcum powder during diaper changes. Talc is harmful to lungs if inhaled. Use cornstarch powder, or just do without.
- Always put your child to bed in pajamas, not day attire. Federal regulations requires that children's sleepwear be fire-resistant; those rules do not apply to daytime clothing.

191

- When you can, select clothing that uses zippers and snaps for closures, instead of buttons. Buttons can be pulled off and swallowed.
- Avoid jackets with drawstrings that dangle from the hood. Any long cord attached to clothing can be a strangulation hazard.

LIVING AREAS

- Even if your Two-Year-Old is a stable walker, it's best to keep wobbly little tables and TV trays out of living areas for the time being. Remove heavy objects from high tables and shelves. If your television set is on a cart, check it for stability.
- Be careful with tablecloths and fabric runners that hang over the ends of tables. Anything that dangles from a table will almost certainly get pulled off—along with whatever is on it.
- Shield electrical outlets, as above, and move lamp cords to the back of tables out of the way. You may need to tape or tack the cords to the underside of the table.
- Use safety gates at the top AND bottom of stairs, at least until you are sure your toddler can manage the stairs safely. Limit the use of spring pressure gates to convenience use, not safety use. They are less secure than attached gates.
- Don't forget the posts along the side of the stairs and on landings. Use Plexiglas panels to screen them.
- Put nonskid pads under area rugs, and NEVER place rugs at tops of stairs.
- Put decals on the glass in sliding and French doors.

- Open double-hung windows from the top only. Or get window locks that limit how far a window can be opened.
- When you're opening or closing a door, keep your child's fingers away from the door hinge side, as well as the latch side. Fingers are easily pinched between the door and the doorjamb, and by the hinges themselves.
- Immobilize swinging doors with a screen-door–type hook placed out of reach. Two-Year-Olds may not be agile enough to use them without getting bumped when the door swings back.
- If you have hard-surface floors, socks can be a slipping hazard. Bare feet are safer on these surfaces.
- Store sewing baskets, knitting supplies, and adult craft items safely out of reach.
- Cigarettes, lighters, and ashtrays must be kept away from your toddler. Children have been known to eat cigarettes and cigarette butts. Remember that tobacco is toxic.
- NEVER leave lighters where children can find them.
- The same goes for the igniter you use for lighting the fire or barbecue grill.
- Even if your child can't yet strike a match, she may eat one. Keep them out of reach.
- Avoid older wooden accordion-type folding play yards; the V-shaped openings at the top are big enough to catch a child's neck. Sides of playpens should be at least twenty inches high.

TOYS

- Pay careful attention to age recommendation on toy packages. When it says it's not recommended for children under Three, there's a good reason—usually because the toy contains small parts that toddlers could swallow or choke on. You are the best judge of when your child is old enough to play with small toys.
- Don't ignore those recommendations just because your Two-Year-Old is precocious. She may be bright, but she could still choke on something small. One Two-Year-Old learned his entire alphabet—except for the letter "I." His parents had given him a magnetic alphabet set for his birthday, but they removed the "I" because it was too small for him to play with safely.
- Beware of toys with small parts, sharp points, or toxic paint. Be on the alert for marbles that may have come from an older child's game.
- Purchase a "truncated cylinder test tube," a simple plastic gadget that sizes toys or pieces of toys. If the toy is small enough to pass through the cylinder, it is small enough to be swallowed.
- Never let your Two-Year-Old play with uninflated balloons or pieces of broken balloons. They are a serious choking hazard.
- Thoroughly examine borrowed, second-hand or hand-me-down toys. They may have splinters, sharp edges or peeling paint. Or they may be of an earlier, more dangerous design.

KITCHEN

- Remember that it's impossible to make a kitchen entirely safe for a Two-Year-Old, so never leave your child alone here.
- Make sure you have a functional smoke alarm and fire extinguisher.
- When you're cooking, keep pot handles turned toward the back of the stove.
- Keep kitchen trash in a covered, latched container. Empty it frequently, and take dangerous disposal items, like cleaning supplies and broken glass, directly to the outside trash bins. Even then, wrap broken glass in layers of newspaper.
- Store cleaning supplies in a locked cabinet.
- Remove mousetraps and insect baits from your home. Use an alternative method of controlling pests until your child is older.
- Never store anything that isn't food in a food or drink container.
- Store plastic bags and plastic- and aluminum-wrap cartons out of your child's reach. Plastic bags can be lethal for toddlers who may put them over their faces and suffocate. And wrap cartons have sharp, serrated blades that can cause injury.
- Never leave a large bucket unattended with liquid in it. Toddlers have been known to topple head-first into buckets and drown.
- If the knobs on your stove are within easy reach of

your toddler, remove them and keep them where only you can reach them.

- Keep cupboard latches and drawer latches on any storage area that you don't specifically want your child to get at.
- Keep electrical appliances unplugged when not in use.
- Your child's high chair should be sturdy, stable, and equipped with a good safety belt. It should be equipped with a latch that keeps it from folding accidentally.
- Keep the high chair away from the stove and other kitchen hazards.
- Don't permit your child to stand in the high chair. If she does it anyway, take her out of the chair.
- Unplug the iron as soon as you're through. Put the hot iron someplace out of the way to cool. Even when it's cool, don't leave it on the board. Ironing boards are wobbly, and irons—even cool ones—are heavy. When the ironing is finished, store the ironing board. Any folding furniture constitutes a pinching hazard.

BATHROOM

- The bathroom, like the kitchen, cannot be completely safe. So always be there with your child.
- Never leave a bathing toddler, even for a moment.
- Use nonslip stickers on the bottom of the bathtub, or a rubber mat with suction cups. Press the mat down to make sure the cups are gripping before putting your child in the tub. Replace the mat if it has holes or tears; loose pieces could be swallowed.
- A spout cover pads the spout and provides some protection if it gets hot.

- Faucet guards (especially on the hot faucet) prevent your child from turning on the water.
- Remove the inside-door locking knob. Replace with a screen-door hinge lock, installed high on the door for adult use.
- Use a locking medicine cabinet for medicine, cleaning supplies, and razors, or move them to a cupboard that can be locked.
- The toilet can present a drowning hazard. Top-heavy toddlers can fall in head-first. Keep the lid down, and forbid playing in the toilet. If necessary, install a lid lock.
- Have ground fault circuit interrupters (GFCIs) installed in place of regular electrical outlets to protect against electrocution when appliances are used near water.
- Never use an electrical appliance, like a shaver or curling iron, while your Two-Year-Old is in the bathtub.
- Most mouthwash contains alcohol and can be harmful if swallowed. Store that with medicine, rather than out on the counter with your toothpaste.

OUTDOORS

- You will need to supervise your toddler outdoors at all times. Even if you've thoroughly childproofed your yard, you never know when a raccoon will wander in, hornets will nest, or toadstools will sprout.
- Recognize poisonous leaves, berries, and mushrooms, and irritants like poison ivy and poison oak. Remove them from the areas where your child will play.
- Teach your child to ask you about any interesting ber-

ries or mushrooms she finds growing in the yard, but never to touch or taste them without asking.

- Toddlers are more susceptible to sunburn than older children and adults. Minimize the amount of time your child will be exposed to intense sunlight. Use sunscreen, but keep it off her fingers—fingers go in mouths.
- Use zinc oxide on her nose and other sensitive spots.
- Don't forget to cover outdoor electrical outlets.
- Make certain areas off-limits: trash can storage, lawn mower, garden shed. Garden and insect pesticides, clippers, trimmers, etc., must be locked away.
- Don't allow your child to ride with you on a riding lawn mower. It's best to keep your child out of the area entirely when the lawn is being mowed.
- Keep your toddler away from the barbecue grill while it is being used, and even after—until it cools down completely.
- Animal feces can harbor disease, and toddlers, who put their hand in their mouths, are susceptible. Remove dog and cat droppings; if your child has a sandbox, fit it with a cover to keep cats from using it as a litter box.
- Beware of stinging insects. Your toddler is most likely to be stung if she steps on a bee, or drinks from a cup of juice that has attracted a yellow jacket.
- If your child is stung by an insect, watch for signs of an allergic reaction. Seek medical attention if she develops severe swelling, itching, nausea, or breathing problems.
- If you use insect repellent, avoid the varieties that contain diethyltoluamide (DEET).

- If ticks are present in your area, check your child regularly after a session outdoors and learn how to remove ticks safely. Don't forget to check her scalp as well.
- Make sure all play equipment is age-appropriate. If you have older children who use slides, swings, croquet sets and such, you'll have to set ground rules and supervise closely.

AROUND WATER

- If you have a swimming pool, be constantly vigilant. Drowning is the third most frequent cause of accidental death among children.
- Be even more vigilant when visiting a home that has a pool, when you have just moved into a new home with a pool, and when you have visitors who may forget to keep gates latched and doors locked.
- Install a fence that is at least four feet high and is fitted with a child-resistant, self-locking gate. The fence should not have openings that could be used as footholds for climbing.
- It's safer to fence the pool separately; do not have direct access from the house to the pool area.
- While you are in the pool with your child, do not rely on inflated toys and flotation devices. They are not foolproof.
- Always have your child wear a child-sized life jacket in a boat. Do not make do with an adult-size flotation device; toddlers can slip out. If you or the boat do not have the proper equipment, stay on shore.

IN THE CAR

- Never, ever allow your toddler to ride in a car without being restrained in an approved car seat. For most Two-Year-Olds, that is still a standard, forward-facing car seat suitable for children up to forty pounds.
- You should already have a car seat. If you buy a new one, buy only an approved seat with a sticker that says it meets all safety standards and was made after 1982 (the year federal safety standards went into effect).
- Explain the reasons for using the seat to your child, but make it clear that it's one rule she does not have a choice about.
- Use your own seat belt. Not only does it protect you and set a good example, but it enables you to maintain better control of your car if you are in an accident.
- In warm weather, cover the car seat with a towel or blanket to keep metal parts from getting painfully hot. Feel the parts before putting your toddler in her car seat.
- After you've buckled her in securely, ask her to put her hands on her head before closing the door. This eliminates the possibility of little fingers getting slammed in the door.
- If your car has childproof door locks and window controls, use them. There have been cases of fatal injuries to toddlers who catch their neck in power windows.
- Always check around your car before getting in and backing out of the garage or driveway. Know where your toddler is. If she is outdoors, make sure you can

SEE her and that she is away from the car before you back up.
- Teach your toddler suitable car behavior. It's hard to concentrate on your driving when your child is shrieking, writhing around, or throwing things.
- *Never* leave your toddler alone in a parked car.

OUT IN THE WORLD

- If you take your Two-Year-Old on bike rides, make sure she's buckled into a sturdy carrier and wearing a properly fitting bicycle helmet.
- Teach your Two-Year-Old to keep a respectful distance from dogs she doesn't know well.
- At shopping malls and other crowded places, use a stroller or hold your child's hand firmly. Don't let her wander off.
- Pick up your toddler and carry her on escalators.
- When you travel, assemble a safety "kit" and take it along. Include a few outlet covers and portable door latches, along with first aid supplies, including syrup of ipecac. Don't forget a nightlight.

POISONING HAZARDS

Toddlers behave impulsively and will taste and swallow just about anything, so don't count on the fact that something smells or tastes awful to slow them down.

- Poison Control numbers should be posted where they're

easy to see when you're in a panic. Include them also on emergency phone lists you give to your sitter.

- Make sure all your medications come with childproof caps. Don't be tempted to leave them open.
- Do not give your child aspirin as a nonprescription pain reliever. In children, aspirin has been linked to Reye's Syndrome, an often-fatal condition.
- Keep syrup of ipecac on hand at all times, but DO NOT give it to your child unless instructed to do so by your doctor or by emergency personnel. Ipecac induces vomiting, and is a life-saver when vomiting is the desired treatment. It should not be used with caustic poisons.
- Be careful of medications you carry in your purse or jacket pocket. Remind guests to put purses in an out-of-the-way place.
- Get rid of houseplants that are toxic, among them the philodendron, dieffenbachia, caladium, pothos, and English ivy.
- Consider decorating with artificial plants during holidays for a few years. Real holly and mistletoe have poisonous berries. Poinsettia plants, while not actually toxic, contain a skin irritant.

GENERAL TIPS

- Buy your toddler a red, or other very brightly colored, jacket, as "reverse camouflage." You'll be able to spot her easier in the yard, or if she gets away from you in a crowd.
- At home, when two parents are taking turns supervising a toddler, be specific about who is watching her.

Don't assume the other parent knows you have gone inside to answer the phone.

- Use a magnetic bulletin board, rather than a cork one. Push pins fall on the floor and can cause injury; thumbtacks land point up and can be stepped on.
- Have operating smoke detectors in use at all times.
- If you own a firearm, follow all safety precautions to the letter. Keep the weapon unloaded, and all ammunition locked away.
- Keep a cordless phone handy. Many toddler disasters occur when a parent leaves the child unattended, "just for a minute," to answer the phone.
- Be careful with places where your toddler might get stuck or trapped: closets that don't open from the inside, trunks, cupboards, locker freezers, even large ice chests. Keep these hazards out of reach or locked, or remove the doors.

And finally: Remember, never count on a rule to protect your Two-Year-Old. Teach her safety rules, but always back them up with your eternal vigilance.

QUESTIONS AND ANSWERS

Q: *What should I do when my toddler refuses to get into her car seat? Sometimes she stiffens up like a board and pushes against the seat belt and I can't get it buckled.*

A: This is one conflict you can't let her win because it's a matter of life and death. It's better to be late than risk your child's life by allowing her to ride unrestrained.

One technique is to let the toddler climb into the seat and belt herself in as much as she is able. In this way, you gradually make her a partner, rather than an adversary. If you try this, ALWAYS check, yourself, to make sure the belt is properly buckled and the straps fit snugly.

You can also take advantage of the Two-Year-Old's love of routine. She will, eventually, take comfort in the sameness of the ritual: we get in the car, we all buckle up, then Mommy starts the car, then we go. You might also harness her love of imitation: She can buckle her teddy bear in an available seat belt; she will probably soon start to lecture Teddy about the importance of buckling up.

Don't start the car engine until everyone is properly buckled. Get in the habit of doing this when you're preparing for a pleasant outing—to the park, or on vacation, or to the frozen yogurt store—rather than when you're late for work. Many small children get so used to this that they believe there's a mechanical reason why the car won't start unless everyone is buckled.

Q: *I have a neighbor who is much more casual about safety rules than I am. She doesn't watch her son as closely as I would, and there's an old shed in her yard that's full of splinters. What should I do when she asks my son over to play with hers?*

A: Safety is more important than politeness. If you genuinely feel your son is at risk of injury if he plays at your neighbor's, then don't permit it. Or, you can let the two boys play there only when you go, too, to keep a close watch on him.

Sooner or later, your son will go out into the world. He'll have to learn to handle splinters and other hazards eventually. But he doesn't have to just yet. He's still little, and your first priority is to keep him safe and sound.

Q: *My son won't stay with me in public places, like stores and carnivals. He always darts away and I'm always always hearing his description over the P.A. system. How can I get him to stay with me?*

A: Two is a peak year for "lost" children, although they are usually not lost for long. However, there are real hazards out there, from accidents to abductions. Your son's running away is a safety issue, rather than an obedience issue, and you'll need to give it top priority. You may have to hold his hand all the time, and let him know that you'll continue to hold on until he's old enough to stay next to you on his own. If he continues to squirm out of your grasp, you'll have to resort to keeping him in a stroller or using a child harness in public or dangerous places.

CONCLUSION

Looking Ahead

Your Two-Year-Old will not be Two for long. Whether that thought inspires a sigh of nostalgia or a sigh of relief, the truth is that your little one is standing on the brink of true childhood. He is leaving his toddler period behind him.

Throughout the last twelve months, he has strengthened his body through his constant activity, and his mind through endless observation and ceaseless questions. He has learned to talk—if not entirely like an adult, then not like an infant either.

He has come to terms with his individuality, a milestone he signals by referring to himself as "I." And as an individual, he has been working to forge new ways of relating to his family, to other children, and to other adults.

He is more independent now, and can manage more and more of his own care. He may have given up diapers, or be about to. He can dress himself, to an extent, and feed himself with a spoon and fork.

In a whole range of ways, he is becoming a civilized

little person. He is more willing to follow house rules, to behave in ways that please you. He can draw a humble picture and entertain you with a song.

In the year ahead, these accomplishments will move him more than ever into the world of people and ideas. At Three, he will strengthen his ability to reason, to think symbolically, to ponder his own feelings and consider the feelings of others. He will be easier to manage, easier to take places, more companionable than he was at Two. He will be sweet, funny, curious, and eager to be part of the world and all its wonders.

As your child celebrates his Third birthday, he will enjoy the candles and the cake as he did last year, but there will be something different this time. This birthday may be one of the earliest memories that he is able to recall throughout his life.

You stand with him on the brink of his ability to remember his childhood, to have a history. Next year, you will write that history together as the magic continues.

Janet Poland is a writer, poet, and former newspaper editor who has written extensively about families and children for newspapers and magazines.

She graduated from Grinnell College and earned a graduate degree in political science from the University of Wisconsin. She worked in state government and in public television before beginning a career in journalism. For more than a decade, she was a reporter, columnist, and editor on the staff of daily newspapers in Pennsylvania, and received numerous journalism awards. More recently, as a freelance journalist, her work has appeared frequently in the *Philadelphia Inquirer*.

She lives in Bucks County, Pennsylvania, with her husband and two sons.

Judi Craig, Ph.D., has counseled thousands of parents and children in more than twenty-seven years as a clinical psychologist. Readers are delighted with the common-sense approach of her most recent books, *Little Kids, Big Questions* and *Parents on the Spot*. Her "Parent Skills" column was featured for eight years in the Sunday *San Antonio Light*; her new column "Family Matters" appears in *Images*, a Sunday magazine in the *San Antonio Express News*. She has also been a consultant to corporations, agencies, schools, and psychiatric hospitals, and recently completed her training as a Master Practitioner in Neurolinguistic Programming. She is a frequent guest on national radio and television. Dr. Craig the mother of three grown children, and lives in San Antonio, Texas.

Understanding what's happening emotionally and physically as your little one evolves from a baby into a child is a vital part of being an effective parent. In these helpful, down-to-earth guides, you'll learn what to expect and what to do at every stage of development. Filled with caring advice, *The Magical Years* helps you keep up with all of the many changes you'll encounter during this special time in your child's life.

THE MAGICAL YEARS

Janet Poland

GETTING TO KNOW YOUR ONE-YEAR-OLD
_____ 95418-2 $4.99 U.S./$5.99 Can.

SURVIVING YOUR TWO-YEAR-OLD
_____ 95582-0 $4.99 U.S./$5.99 Can.

MAKING FRIENDS WITH YOUR THREE-YEAR-OLD
_____ 95627-4 $4.99 U.S./$5.99 Can.

CHILD CARE BOOKS
YOU CAN
COUNT ON—

from ST. MARTIN'S PAPERBACKS